150 Letters that Get Results

150 Letters that Get Results

Ashley Holmes

 CONSUMERS' ASSOCIATION

Which? Books are commissioned by
Consumers' Association and published by
Which? Ltd, 2 Marylebone Road,
London NW1 4DF
Email address: books@which.net

Distributed by The Penguin Group:
Penguin Books Limited, 27 Wrights Lane, London W8 5TZ

First edition (published as *120 Letters that Get Results*) October 1991
Reprinted January and July 1992
Revised edition September 1992
Reprinted July 1993
Revised edition May 1995
Revised edition June 1996
150 Letters that Get Results first published March 1997
Revised edition April 1998
Reprinted January 1999

British Library Cataloguing in Publication Data
A catalogue record for this book is available from the British Library

ISBN 0 85202 737 0

Help at hand

If you have ever been faced with the sort of problems described in this
book, you'll be glad to know that *Which?* has a service, open to all,
whereby you can consult one of the UK's top consumer lawyers by
telephone at any time Monday–Friday (9 am–5 pm). For details of how to
subscribe to *Which?* Legal Service, either write to *Which?*, Gascoyne Way,
Hertford X, SG14 1LH, telephone free on 0800 252100 or visit website
www.which.net. Information about other *Which?* books, *Which?* and its
sister magazines can be obtained from the same address.

Cover and text design by Kyzen Creative Consultants

Typeset by FMT Colour Limited
Printed and bound in Great Britain by Clays Ltd, Bungay, Suffolk

Contents

How to use this book

150 Letters that Get Results shows you how to make a written complaint in the most effective way, using a standard letter which you can adapt to suit your own problem and which employs the most appropriate phrasing and legal terminology.

To get the most out of this book, read the Introduction carefully before you put pen to paper. It gives a basic summary of consumer rights and explains the key pieces of legislation.

The Introduction also takes you through the practical sequence of making a complaint, from the initial notification to the last resort, going to court. It is essential to bear in mind the advice it gives on managing your complaint – keeping records of telephone conversations and copies of all correspondence, for example – and on the elements of an effective letter, such as citing relevant legislation, using correct legal vocabulary and setting deadlines. All are components of a successful campaign to achieve what you want.

Once you have read the Introduction, consult the relevant chapter for your problem. If, for example, you are in dispute with a shop over a defective hair-dryer, turn to Chapter 1: *Buying Goods*, and then read the text preceding the standard letters. This gives further advice regarding your rights and how to pursue them. Once you have digested this information, use the appropriate standard letter to address your problem.

Each letter has a title explaining to whom you should send it. Further, each one has been constructed to allow you to insert specific information where relevant – instructions to do this are given in square brackets throughout. It is important to remember that you are communicating in written form a fact that is often a visual one, so aim for clarity – say something like 'the on-off switch became loose, and the hair-dryer emitted blue sparks and a burning smell'.

The next paragraph generally advises the recipient of the legal basis of your claim and the obligations you are owed, again with elements for you to complete. The final paragraph sets a timetable for a response. The whole letter shows that you intend to pursue the matter, and its tone, though formal and polite, is firm.

Should the recipient deny your claim, you should then use the subsequent letter and, can, if necessary, carry out your threat of instigating court action by following the guidelines in Chapter 17: *Going to Court*.

All the letters in this book can be adapted to individual cases as required, and you will be advised of those circumstances in which it is appropriate to make 'time of the essence' or to head your correspondence 'without prejudice'. You will also be warned of situations in which it is essential to seek professional legal advice.

Throughout this book, for 'he' read 'he or she'.

Introduction

WHAT can you do if your new car goes badly wrong but the garage refuses to take it back? What should you do if the work you have just had done in your kitchen is not up to standard, or you are in dispute with an electricity company because you think your bill is too high? Perhaps your holiday did not live up to the glowing description in the tour operator's brochure. How do you go about obtaining satisfaction? When something goes wrong with the goods or services you have bought, it is likely to be time-consuming and possibly expensive to get matters put right.

To make a successful complaint, you need to know your legal rights as a consumer. You also need to know how to complain effectively: approaching the right person and setting out your claim in the right way, using appropriate language and stating your case clearly will increase your prospects of success and redress. This introduction summarises the law governing consumer problems and provides detailed advice on putting together a fruitful letter of complaint. From time to time you may need to use the vocabulary of legislation, which has precise meaning and may imply more than is immediately obvious to a lay person – see the Glossary at the back of the book for explanations to the key words and phrases.

Your rights – a summary

Before making a complaint, make sure you know exactly what you want to achieve. Do you want money – a refund or compensation? Do you simply want an apology from the person or organisation to whom you are complaining? Whatever it is you are seeking should be made clear from the outset. You should also be certain of your legal rights. When something goes wrong with the goods you have bought, or services are not up to scratch, knowing your rights as a consumer puts you in a stronger position to resolve the problem to your advantage. The basics of consumer law are explained below, while subsequent chapters provide further details of your rights in specific circumstances.

Buying goods

Every time you buy goods from a shop, street market, mail order company or any other kind of supplier, you enter into a contract with the seller. A contract is an agreement defined by law, and gives you certain legal rights. Under the Sale of Goods Act 1979 as amended by the Sale and Supply of Goods Act 1994 the goods must:

- **fit the description** used in any advertisement, label, packaging and so on relating to them – the year or make, type, colour, size or materials used, for example, must all be accurately described.
- **be of satisfactory quality** – the goods should work properly, have no major or minor defects, be safe, and, if new, look new and be in good condition.
- **be fit for their purpose** – if you made it clear to the retailer when choosing goods that you needed them for a specific purpose, they must fulfil those requirements.

If goods you have bought do not meet these requirements, the retailer is under a legal obligation to sort out your problem. You may be able to reject the goods and get your money back. You must act quickly – in law, you only have a 'reasonable time' after buying in which to reject the goods. Although this period is not defined in the relevant legislation, it is usually a relatively short period and, depending on the item, can be as little as a few weeks. After a reasonable time has elapsed, it is too late for you to reject the goods and obtain a full refund. However, you are still legally entitled to receive compensation for faulty goods, and in practice compensation usually amounts to the cost of repair. If it is too late to get a cash refund, it may be worth agreeing to accept a free repair or new replacement. Otherwise, you may have a claim under a guarantee given with the product.

Some special cases

Delivery times

If it is clear that the goods you have ordered are required by a specific date, such as Christmas cards, and they do not arrive in time, you are entitled to cancel your order and to get your money back. And if you have to pay more to buy the goods elsewhere, you can demand the difference in price from the initial supplier.

If no delivery date is fixed, the supplier is under a legal obligation to send the goods within a reasonable time. If you need to receive the goods by a specific date, let the supplier know in writing that 'time is of the essence' and set a date for delivery. By doing so, you make the delivery date an important term of the legally binding contract between you.

Mail order

You may have extra protection under the codes of practice governing mail order purchases, so check with the relevant trade associations (see Addresses at the back of this book). If you pay with order in response to an advertisement which carries the appropriate logo and which appears in a national newspaper that is a member of the Mail Order Protection Scheme (MOPS), and the company to which you sent your order goes into liquidation, you can reclaim your money through that scheme. But you cannot do so if the advertiser does not have the MOPS 'seal of approval'.

Credit

Whether you pay for faulty goods or services in cash or by credit card, your claim for redress is against the seller. But paying by credit card, such as Access or Visa, gives you the added protection of the Consumer Credit Act 1974, provided the goods cost over £100. If you pay by this means, then along with the seller, the credit card company is also liable for the faulty goods or services. This is useful if, for example, the retailer goes bust (see page 149).

If you buy on credit through a hire purchase agreement, credit sale or conditional sale, the finance company, *not* the seller, is responsible to you for the quality of the goods. You also have more time in which to reject goods on hire purchase (see page 149).

Private purchases

When you buy goods from a private individual, the only responsibilities on the seller are that he or she must own the goods and that the goods must correspond with any description you have been given. So if you buy a car from a private advertisement in a newspaper, you cannot complain if it breaks down after a week unless it was described, for example, as being in perfect working order.

Retail cut-price sales

If you buy goods at reduced prices in a sale, you still retain all your rights under the Sale of Goods Act. However, if you are buying goods described as 'seconds', be certain to find out before you buy them exactly what defect makes them not of first quality. Notices in shops to the effect that no refunds are made on sale goods have no basis in law – if the goods are faulty, you are entitled to a refund.

Services

When you ask someone to carry out a service for you, such as building work, plumbing or dry-cleaning, you enter a legally binding contract which gives you basic legal rights. As well as the right to receive the service that is defined in the terms of the contract (types of materials that will be used, dates by which the work will be done, and so on), you also have legal rights implied into the contract. The Supply of Goods and Services Act 1982 (common law in Scotland) states that the work covered by the contract must be carried out with reasonable skill and care. It also says that if the contract does not specify precise dates or prices, the work must be carried out within a reasonable time and for a reasonable price. Again, 'reasonable' is not always clearly defined, but usually depends upon whether or not another supplier would have done the same as the firm you are claiming against.

If something goes wrong as the result of a service – your new plaster starts to crack, or the roof which you had mended still leaks – first ask the contractor to put the defects right. If the contractor will not do so, you are legally entitled to employ another to rectify the problem – and then ask the first contractor to foot the bill.

Other important consumer legislation

Other legislation conferring individual consumer rights includes:

Arbitration Act 1996, and, in Scotland, the Consumer Arbitration Agreements Act 1984

If the disputed sum falls within the limits for the small claims court, currently £3,000 in England and Wales, consumers are not legally bound by clauses in contracts which state that any dispute must be referred to arbitration; they have the choice of court *or* arbitration.

Consumer Credit Act 1974

This regulates credit agreements and gives purchasers a number of rights: advertisements for credit schemes must show true rates of interest without hidden extras; purchasers have certain rights to pay off the debt before the time stipulated in the agreement; purchasers who sign a credit agreement at home have a cooling-off period during which they may change their mind and cancel the agreement.

Consumer Protection Act 1987, and, in Northern Ireland, the (N.I.) Order 1987

This states that: (1) manufacturers are strictly liable if the products they make are defective and cause personal injury, or damage to your property over £250; (2) all goods must comply with a general safety requirement; and (3) bogus bargain offers are controlled.

Consumer Protection (Cancellation of Contracts Concluded Away from Business Premises) Regulations 1987

This gives purchasers a seven-day cooling-off period during which they have the right to cancel certain contracts made during an unrequested visit by a salesman to their home even when they are not buying on credit.

Occupiers' Liability Act 1957

This gives people the right to claim compensation if they are injured due to negligence while visiting someone's premises.

Misrepresentation Act 1967, and, in Northern Ireland, the Misrepresentation Act (N.I.) 1967

If consumers enter an agreement on the basis of a statement purporting to be a fact but which turns out to be untrue, they have the right to cancel the deal and get their money back if they act quickly, or to compensation. The Act does not apply to Scotland. However, Scottish law is broadly similar.

Sale and Supply of Goods Act 1994

This law updates the Sale of Goods Act 1979. It replaces the outdated phrase 'merchantable quality' with 'satisfactory quality' and generally gives consumers improved rights.

Supply of Goods (Implied Terms) Act 1973

This defines purchasers' rights when buying on hire purchase: the goods must correspond to their description, be of satisfactory quality and reasonably fit for their purpose.

Unfair Contract Terms Act 1977

The small print in contracts for the sale of goods cannot take away purchasers' rights under the Sale of Goods Act. These and other notices or conditions in contracts which exclude or restrict liability for financial loss or damage to property have to be fair and reasonable. If they are not, they will be invalid under the Act and will not affect a claim.

Unfair Terms in Consumer Contracts Regulations 1994

The Unfair Terms in Consumer Contracts Regulations 1994 set out new law on unfair contract terms. The Regulations cover consumer contracts with businesses made after 1 July 1995. They add to and do not replace existing protection for consumers, particularly that provided by the Unfair Contract Act 1977.

Unsolicited Goods and Services Act 1971

This gives recipients of unrequested and unwanted goods the right to get rid of them without paying for them.

Criminal laws

Certain criminal laws also affect consumers. Although they do not entitle consumers to get compensation directly, reporting a criminal offence will provide support for the complaint. The most relevant laws are:

The Consumer Protection Act 1987

This stipulates that only safe goods should be put on sale and prohibits misleading price indications.

The Food Safety Act 1990

This covers food standards and hygiene wherever food is manufactured, prepared or sold, as well as other aspects of food and drink.

Trade Descriptions Act 1968

This makes it a criminal offence for traders to make false statements about the goods they sell.

How to make an effective complaint

If you discover a defect in goods soon after purchase, act quickly. Insist on speaking to the manager of the establishment where you bought them or to someone else in authority who can make a decision about the problem. Addressing your complaint to the right person is more likely to resolve the problem to your satisfaction.

Keep a record of verbal complaint

You may of course complain in person initially, but if you complain by telephone make sure you have a pen and some paper to hand so that you can keep a record of the conversation. In either case, always ascertain the name and position of the person to whom you are speaking. Write these down, together with the date and details of your conversation. Your records of such conversations will be important if you have to take your claim further.

Send a letter of complaint

Unless your problem is resolved immediately, follow up your verbal complaint by a letter. Address it to the person immediately responsible for sorting out the problem, having ascertained his or her name and position. By sending your letter to a named individual you reduce the chance of it being passed round the organisation and perhaps being ignored or lost. The letter should ideally be typed. If this is not possible, write as neatly as possible to ensure legibility. Always date letters. It also makes sense, especially when dealing with large organisations like insurance companies and tour operators, to give the letter a heading such as the name and number of your insurance policy, your holiday booking reference and so on. Use this heading, and any reference given to you by the organisation, every time you write.

As we advise you to ascertain the name of the person to whom you address your complaint, we recommend the use of 'Yours sincerely' in the letters in this book. In instances where you do not know the addressee's name, use 'Yours faithfully'.

Keep to the point

Keep your letter brief, with short paragraphs setting out the details of your problem. Stick to the facts, making sure they are correct (model number of the goods, date of purchase, the nature of the defect etc.). Avoid repetition. Do not make personal remarks in your letter, however justified they may seem to be. Keep your letter polite and never lose your temper – this will not help your claim and may make it more difficult to settle the problem. But you should be firm.

State the legal basis of your claim

Let the person to whom you are complaining know the legal basis of your claim, and, if possible, include brief details of the relevant piece of law covering your case. Mentioning the Sale of Goods Act 1979 if you are complaining about faulty goods or the Supply of Goods and Services Act 1982 in respect of inadequate services, for example, shows that you are aware of your rights and mean business.

State what redress you are seeking

Be clear about what you want to achieve and specify what you want from the other party, whether it is your money refunded, a repair or a replacement of the defective item. If you want financial compensation, spell out why and state the exact sum that you expect to receive. Bear in mind that while you have legal rights to redress you are also under a legal obligation to keep your claim as small as is reasonably possible.

Set a deadline

Set a deadline by which you want a response from the other party. Be reasonable and do not give too short a period of time for the individual or organisation to respond appropriately. If it is a simple matter of giving you a refund, 14 days is a reasonable time in which to expect your letter to be answered and the cheque sent. If you want repairs done to faulty building work, such as a leaky new roof, a longer deadline for a response would be appropriate, because the builder may be committed to carry out other jobs in the near future and may need time to make suitable arrangements to put your problem right.

Stick to deadlines

You should keep to the time limits that you have imposed on the other party. That way your claim will be taken more seriously by the person or organisation to whom you are complaining.

You should also watch out for any time limits set out in specific complaints procedures. For example, insurance claims, and claims for compensation for luggage lost or damaged by airlines, have to be made within specific time limits. If you leave it too late to complain, you may lose your right to compensation.

Use recorded delivery

Send important letters by recorded delivery – you get a record of posting and a signature is obtained by the postman on delivery. This will prevent the other party claiming not to have received your letter.

Get evidence

Once you have decided to write, collect any evidence you can to support your claim: invoices, receipts, holiday brochures and confirmation invoices (if you are complaining about a holiday), advertisements, estimates, bills, the names and addresses of witnesses, car registration numbers (if you are making an insurance claim) and so on. Photographs of any damage that has been caused – from a leaky roof or cracked kettle – or, for example, of dirty holiday accommodation, can also help your case. If appropriate, obtain written evidence from an independent technical expert in the trade concerned and written confirmation from witnesses of what they saw, heard and experienced. If your complaint is disputed, you will have to prove your case, and evidence in support of your claim, particularly expert evidence, may well tip the balance of the argument in your favour.

Keep copies of relevant documents

Do not send original documents with your letters. Send photocopies and keep the originals in a safe place in case you need to produce them at a later date. Take care not to add further damage to the items which are the object of your complaint. When you discover that goods are faulty, stop using them immediately, particularly if you want to get rid of them and claim a refund.

Always keep a copy of your letters – you may need to refer to them later if you are unable to settle your dispute easily and have to take further action such as using an arbitration scheme, referring the matter to an ombudsman or, in the last resort, taking the case to court.

Be persistent

If you fail to get what you want at your first attempt, be persistent: write another letter of complaint setting out your dissatisfaction. Your first letter of complaint may not be enough to get your problem resolved. So be firm and show that you mean business – that way you are more likely to get redress. Do not fall prey to attempts to fob you off with less than you are entitled to, such as:

'We do not guarantee products' This has no basis in law. Your rights as a consumer apply whether you have a written guarantee or not.

'It is not our problem. Try the manufacturer' This is not true. Your contract is with the trader who supplied the goods or services and that party is legally obliged to put things right.

'We do not give refunds' This statement is not supported by consumer legislation. If the goods you have bought are not as described, of satisfactory quality, or fit for their purpose, you are entitled to a refund if you act quickly enough. Notices saying 'No refunds given' are against the law. Report shops displaying them to your local Trading Standards Department.

'You are too late. You should have complained within 30 days' Do not accept time limits of this sort. Whether you are complaining about goods or services, even if it is too late to get a full refund (i.e. the 'reasonable' period of time has elapsed), your rights to compensation last for six years (five years in Scotland).

'You caused the problem, not us' You should not be deterred by this kind of tactic. If, for example, the floor you have just had laid in your bathroom starts to warp because of contact with water, do not be put off claiming. Bathroom floors should withstand water and if the flooring does not do so it is not fit for its purpose, so you are entitled to claim. If the problem is not as clear-cut as this, you may need an independent test on the item.

'We cannot do anything without a receipt' Having a receipt is not a legal requirement for obtaining redress. If the trader asks for proof of purchase, a receipt is useful. A credit card voucher, for example, would be legally acceptable.

'No refunds on sale items' Goods bought in a sale are still covered by consumer legislation. If you buy seconds, you cannot expect them to be perfect, but they must still be of satisfactory quality (i.e. free from hidden defects) and as described. But you are not entitled to compensation for any defects which were pointed out to you at point of purchase or which you should have spotted before buying.

Follow the right complaints procedure

You should always adhere to the proper complaints procedure established for your particular problem. Missing out a step in the procedure by complaining to someone inappropriately senior in the organisation or to the wrong body or watchdog may lead to your letters being ignored or redirected, which will cause delay. You may also cause unnecessary antagonism, which may damage your chances of success.

Suppliers of gas and electricity and professions like the law and medicine have their own mechanisms for dealing with complaints. Turn to the relevant chapters later in the book for detailed explanations of these procedures.

Be reasonable when considering an offer

You should be reasonable and be prepared to come to an agreement if you receive a fair offer, even if it is not exactly what you wanted at the outset.

However, you should bear in mind that accepting an offer of compensation normally means that you cannot ask for more later. If you are uncertain about accepting an offer, take legal advice.

To avoid committing yourself by mistake when negotiating figures for a compromise settlement, write 'Without prejudice' at the top of that part of your correspondence. That way those letters cannot be held against you and cannot be revealed if you finally have to go to court to pursue your claim. But do not write 'Without prejudice' on the rest of your letters – those in which you set out and pursue the main basis of your claim, for instance.

Get expert advice

If you need help in pursuing your claim, contact your local Citizens Advice Bureau, consumer advice centre, law centre or, particularly if you have been personally injured, a solicitor. (Some solicitors offer free advice under the Accident Line Service, Freephone (0500) 192939.)

Take formal action

If all else fails, the following courses of action may be open to you:

Court The final stage before initiating court action is to send a 'letter before action', giving notice to the other party that unless you receive redress within a specified period (usually seven days) the matter will be taken to court. The 'small claims' procedure in the county court (sheriff court in Scotland) is a cheap and informal way of dealing with claims up to £5,000 (£1,000 in Northern Ireland, £750 in Scotland). See Chapter 17, Going to court.

Arbitration Various trade and professional bodies offer their own low-cost arbitration schemes. The Chartered Institute of Arbitrators (Arbiters in Scotland) will give an independent decision on your dispute if both you and the other party agree to it. But this can be expensive. If you lose you may have to pay the arbitrator's costs – probably between £50 and £75 per hour. If there is no clear loser, you will have to pay a share of the costs, which again could be considerable.

Ombudsmen These are often classified as either 'public' or 'private' sector and are traditionally seen as a means of resolving disputes between individuals and public or private sector bodies. Examples of the public sector ombudsmen are the Parliamentary Commissioner and the Local Government Ombudsmen. Private ombudsmen cover many service industries, such as insurance, building societies, banking and legal services.

Usually you must take up your claim with the company's head office first. After that, you can apply to the relevant ombudsman to investigate a complaint. The service is free, and if you are not happy with the final decision you can still pursue your claim in the courts.

Chapter 1

Buying goods

THE word 'goods' covers almost everything apart from land – from pets to cars and computer software. Every time you buy goods from a shop, mail-order company, garage or any kind of retailer, you enter into a contract with the seller. This contract gives you certain rights that are backed by the Sale of Goods Act 1979 as amended by the Sale and Supply of Goods Act 1994. For example, it is an implied term that the goods will be of satisfactory quality. In other words, the goods should work properly, be free from minor defects, be safe and, if new, look new and be in good condition. And depending on what it is you are buying, the goods should also last a reasonable amount of time.

If you tell a retailer that you require goods for a specific purpose, then as well as being fit for their more general purpose, the goods should also be fit for that specific purpose. This obligation applies only if you make your requirements clear to the retailer at the point of purchase and if the retailer affirms that the goods will perform that function.

The goods you buy must also match any description given of them – the year of manufacture, the type, the colour, size, component materials and so on. If you can prove that the goods you bought did not meet these requirements at the time of purchase, you have a claim against the retailer for breach of contract.

According to the amended Sale of Goods Act 1979 you have only a 'reasonable' time in which to reject faulty goods and receive a full refund of the purchase price. There no precise legal definition of 'reasonable' – it depends on the circumstances of each case and, in some instances, a reasonable time can be as little as a few weeks. After that period has elapsed you are entitled to compensation only, which usually amounts to the cost of repair. If the goods are still under guarantee, it is probably worthwhile to claim under the manufacturer's guarantee. And remember, guarantees do not take anything away from your rights under the Sale of Goods Act.

So before you initiate your complaint, work out what you are entitled to, and decide whether you want your money back, an exchange, a repair or compensation.

You are not obliged to take faulty goods back to the retailer: you are legally entitled to require the retailer to collect them from you. You should therefore arrange this once you have received the retailer's cheque for the full purchase price.

It is often difficult to show that goods were inherently faulty when purchased if you have had them for some time, but to have a successful claim you will have to prove that that was the case, and you will often need technical evidence from an expert to add weight to your claim. It is, however, important to remember that under your rights laid down by the Sale of Goods Act, the retailer has an obligation towards you for six years from the date of purchase in any instance of breach of contract. This means that even if a reasonable period of time has elapsed, so long as you complain within six years (five years in Scotland) of purchasing the goods you are entitled to compensation.

If you spot a defect in goods straight away, act quickly: contact the retailer (telephone or go back to the shop) and ask to see the manager. Spell out the exact nature of the problem and how you wish it to be resolved. If you do not receive satisfactory redress initially, write to the retailer reiterating your case clearly, giving both full details of defects in the goods and your preferred resolution of the matter. In your letter, establish a time limit for action by the retailer – for example, 14 days in which to refund your money.

If you ask the retailer for a repair, do so while stating that you are reserving your rights under the Sale of Goods Act. By doing so, you retain the right to claim compensation at a later date if the retailer does not carry out a free repair, or if the repair proves to be faulty.

Rejecting a retailer's denial of liability

Some retailers claim that it is not their responsibility to sort out problems with faulty goods and that the responsibility lies with the manufacturer. Do not be fobbed off. Remember that your contract is with the retailer who sold you the goods. Be persistent, and remind the retailer of his legal obligations under the Sale of Goods Act 1979.

Damage caused by faulty goods

You are also entitled to claim under the Sale of Goods Act 1979 for any damage caused by faulty goods. If, for example, your washing machine breaks down and damages clothes that are in it at the time, you are entitled to claim compensation from the retailer for the damaged clothes as well as for the machine. You can claim only if the damage is caused as a direct and foreseeable result of your being supplied with faulty goods. You will need evidence that items were damaged by the faulty goods, so take photographs if you can, and, if possible, keep the damaged items in a safe place until your claim is settled.

Injury caused by faulty goods

The Consumer Protection Act 1987 states that manufacturers (or producers) are strictly liable if the products they make are defective. If you can prove that a defect in a product caused you personal injury, or damage to your property over £250, you can claim compensation from the manufacturer, *not* from the retailer. Anyone so injured can claim – the right to do so is not restricted to the purchaser of the goods.

You are entitled to compensation for the time you have had to take off work, lost wages, and the pain and suffering caused by the injury. The amount of compensation you can claim depends on the seriousness of the injury and the nature of the 'loss of amenity'. If you are a painter and decorator, for example, and cannot use ladders for six months, you will be entitled to claim more compensation than someone who does not have to climb ladders for a living. Get legal advice from a solicitor on how much to claim before initiating your complaint.

Rejecting goods that do not correspond with samples

If you place an order on the basis of samples of the goods which you intend to buy (material for a sofa cover, for example), the finished goods must correspond with that sample. If they do not, you have a claim against the retailer for breach of contract.

Carpets – a particular problem

Some kinds of carpet suffer from 'shading' – they develop patches and marks where the carpet appears discoloured. It occurs when some of the carpet pile lies in a different direction from the rest, producing light and dark patches which will not go away. Carpet retailers sometimes refuse to offer compensation for shading by claiming that it is an innate feature of the carpet that has to be accepted, but you should not be deterred. If the appearance of your carpet is unacceptable, and you were not specifically warned about shading before you purchased the carpet, you have a claim against the retailer under the Sale of Goods Act 1979 for breach of contract.

It often happens that by the time the shading has become apparent, it is too late to reject a carpet which suffers from shading and get your money back, because by the time the problem has manifested itself, a period longer than a reasonable time has elapsed. In many cases your options are restricted to a claim for a replacement carpet.

The late delivery of goods

The law does not normally regard time as a crucial element in contracts for consumer goods. If it is important that the goods you have ordered are delivered to you by a particular date, you should make this clear to the supplier by marking 'time is of the essence' in writing when placing your order. If the goods ordered subsequently do not arrive on time, the supplier is in breach of contract and you are legally entitled to receive a full refund of the price that you paid. And if it costs you more than the price you paid with your order to get the same goods elsewhere, you are also entitled to receive the difference in price from the initial supplier.

If the supplier agrees to deliver the goods but no date for delivery is fixed, the Sale of Goods Act 1979 says that the supplier must send the goods to you within a reasonable time. However, as in other instances, there is no hard-and-fast rule about what is 'reasonable'. It depends on the circumstances – the type of goods, their availability and so on.

Sometimes it is clear, either from a catalogue or from the nature of the goods themselves, that the goods are required by a particular date. If you order goods from a Christmas catalogue, or the goods themselves are particularly seasonal (Christmas cards, say), then it is clear that they must be delivered in time for Christmas. If such goods are not delivered in time, you are entitled to cancel your order and to ask for a full refund of the purchase price.

Mail-order problems

If you order goods through the post or through a mail-order catalogue, you are protected by the amended Sale of Goods Act 1979. The goods should therefore be of satisfactory quality, be reasonably fit for their purpose and should correspond to their description in advertisements or catalogues. If they do not meet these requirements, you have exactly the same rights that you would have if you bought the goods over the counter at a shop.

When buying goods from a catalogue or from an advertisement in a newspaper or magazine, you are probably covered by one of the mail order protection schemes (see Addresses at the back of this book).

The relevant trade associations will usually investigate any complaint against a member who does not abide by the appropriate code of practice, and they will usually conciliate between you and one of their members free of charge. As a last resort, they usually also offer the option of independent arbitration. You can get copies of their codes of practice direct from them.

These associations will also respond to your complaint if a company to whom you have paid money in advance stops trading or goes into liquidation. But there are time limits within which you have to claim, so contact the advertisement manager of the newspaper or magazine which carried the advertisement as soon as possible.

Before placing your order, you should ask the publication

carrying the advertisement whether the appropriate protection schemes will cover you in these circumstances. Keep a copy of the advertisement, too.

Mail-order goods damaged in transit

In practice, mail-order companies which belong to trade associations such as the Mail Order Protection Scheme (MOPS) generally agree to replace goods free of charge if they have been damaged in transit. Check with the association to see what is covered by the relevant scheme. You may also have some comeback against a supplier which is not a member of any trade association. If the supplier cannot prove that the goods left its premises in perfect condition, you have a claim to be reimbursed for the cost of the goods.

If it can be proved that the goods were damaged in transit, you have a claim against the carrier. In the case of the Post Office, you should complete form P58 (available at any post office) and send it to the Head Postmaster. Remember to keep a copy of what you write. If you can show that a parcel was damaged in the post, you are entitled to compensation on a sliding scale, but this may not always reflect your actual loss.

Rejecting defective goods bought from a shop

Dear

[Reference: make and model]

On **[date]** I bought the above **[item]** from your shop. On **[date]** it developed serious defects. **[Describe problems]**.

Section 14 of the amended Sale of Goods Act 1979 requires you to supply goods of satisfactory quality. The fact that the **[item]** showed the above defects **[.....]** days after purchase shows that it was inherently faulty at the time of purchase. You are therefore in breach of contract and I hereby exercise my rights under the Sale of Goods Act to reject the **[item]** and to claim a refund of the full purchase price of **[£.....]** from you.

I look forward to receiving your cheque for this sum within the next 14 days. If you fail to reimburse me I shall have no alternative but to issue a summons against you in the county court for recovery of the money without further reference to you.

Yours sincerely

Asking a retailer for a free repair to defective goods

Dear

[Reference: make and model]

On **[date]** I bought the above **[item]** from your shop. On **[date], [.....]** days after purchase, it developed a serious fault **[describe].**

Section 14 of the amended Sale of Goods Act 1979 requires you to supply goods of satisfactory quality. The problem described above shows there was an inherent defect in the **[item]** at the time of purchase, and that it was not of satisfactory quality. You are therefore in breach of contract.

In these circumstances I am legally entitled to financial compensation. However, while fully reserving my rights under the Sale of Goods Act, I am prepared to give you an opportunity to repair the **[item]** without charge to me. Please inform me in writing of your proposals for effecting this repair within the next 14 days.

Yours sincerely

Rejecting goods that are not fit for their specific purpose

Dear

[Reference: make and model]

On **[date]** I bought the above **[item]** from your shop. Before purchasing it, I told a member of your staff that I needed it for a specific purpose **[describe]**. He selected the above brand and model as being suitable for my requirements. When I tried to use it for that purpose, it proved unsuitable **[describe problem]**.

Section 14 of the amended Sale of Goods Act 1979 requires you to supply goods which are of satisfactory quality and fit for their specific purpose if that purpose is made clear to the retailer at the time of purchase. The problem described above indicates that the **[item]** was not fit for the purpose of **[describe]**, despite your staff's assurances. You are therefore in breach of contract, and I am exercising my rights under the Sale of Goods Act to reject the goods and to receive from you a refund of the full purchase price of **[£.....]**.

I expect to receive your cheque for that amount within 14 days. If you fail to reimburse me I shall have no alternative but to issue a summons against you in the county court for recovery of the money without further reference to you.

Yours sincerely

Rejecting goods that do not match their description

Dear

[Reference: make and model]

On **[date]** I bought the above **[item]** at a cost of **[£.....]** from you.

When I visited your establishment on **[date]** the **[item]** was described to me as follows **[describe]**. It was on the basis of your description that I proceeded with the purchase. I have subsequently discovered that the **[item]** does not match that description and is **[describe including actual value, if appropriate]**.

As your description was a key factor in my decision to buy the **[item]**, the sale was one 'by description', and as the **[item]** does not correspond with that description, you are in breach of contract.

I am therefore exercising my rights under the Sale of Goods Act 1979 to reject the **[item]** and expect you to reimburse me with a refund of the full purchase price of **[£.....]** within 14 days.

If you fail to reimburse me I shall have no alternative but to issue a summons against you in the county court for recovery of the money without further recourse to you.

Yours sincerely

NOTE
Remember, you are not obliged to take or send the goods back to the supplier: you are entitled to ask the supplier to collect them, once you have received the supplier's cheque.

Rejecting a retailer's denial of liability for defective goods

Dear

[Reference: make and model]

I wrote to you on **[date]** about the above defective **[item]** bought from your shop on **[date]**. Your reply of **[date]** denied liability for the defective item, claiming that I should complain to the manufacturer instead.

My claim against you is based on the amended Sale of Goods Act 1979. Section 14 of the Act requires you to supply goods of satisfactory quality. Your failure to supply such goods means that I have a claim against you for breach of contract which is unaffected by any other rights I may have under the guarantee offered by the manufacturer.

I trust that this clarifies the position and I expect to receive your written proposal for arranging for a free repair to the **[item]** within the next seven days.

Yours sincerely

Complaining to a retailer about damage caused by defective goods

Dear

[Reference: make and model]

On **[date]** I bought the above **[item]** from your shop. On **[date]** it developed a serious fault **[describe]** causing damage to my property **[describe]**. This cost **[£.....]** to repair.

Section 14 of the amended Sale of Goods Act 1979 requires you to supply goods which are of satisfactory quality. As the **[item]** is faulty and therefore unsatisfactory, you are in breach of contract.

I am therefore entitled to financial compensation for the faulty goods. However, while fully reserving my rights I am prepared to give you an opportunity to repair the **[item]** without any charge to me.

I am also legally entitled to claim **[£.....]** for the **[above damage]** as this cost arose as a direct result of the **[defect]**.

Please inform me within 14 days of your proposals for effecting repairs to the **[item]**. I also look forward to receiving your cheque for **[£.....]** within 14 days. If you fail to reimburse me I shall have no alternative but to issue a summons against you in the county court for recovery of the money without further reference to you.

Yours sincerely

Informing a retailer that you are claiming a repair to defective goods from a manufacturer, while reserving your rights

Dear

[Reference: make and model]

On **[date]** I bought the above **[item]** from your shop.

When I tried to use the **[item]** on **[date]** I discovered that it was faulty: **[describe]**.

I am sending the **[item]** back to the manufacturer for a free repair according to the terms of its guarantee. However, I reserve my rights under the amended Sale of Goods Act 1979 to reject the **[item]** and claim a refund from you if the manufacturer does not resolve the problem.

Yours sincerely

Complaining to a manufacturer about injury caused by faulty goods

Dear

[Reference: make and model]

On **[date]** I bought the above **[item]** from **[retailer: name and address]**. On **[date]** the **[item]** proved defective, injuring me in the process **[describe]**. The result of the injury was **[describe, together with any consequences, such as absence from work]**.

As the manufacturer of the **[item]** which was inherently defective and which caused my injuries, you are liable to me under the Consumer Protection Act 1987 for the personal injury caused by the defect in your product.

I am taking legal advice about the amount of compensation I should claim and will inform you of how much I am claiming in due course.

Yours sincerely

Rejecting goods that do not correspond with samples

Dear

[Reference: brief description of goods]

On **[date]** the above **[item: describe]** was delivered to me. It is unsatisfactory. My order of **[date]** was placed on the basis of specific samples shown to me **[describe: colour, finish, size etc.]**. The item delivered to me differs from the samples chosen in that it is: **[describe]**.

Since the **[item]** does not correspond with the sample I saw and relied upon when placing my order, you are in breach of contract, and under the Sale of Goods Act 1979 I am legally entitled to reject the **[item]** and to receive from you a refund of the full purchase price of **[£.....]**.

I am therefore exercising my right to do so and I expect to receive your cheque for **[£.....]** within 14 days. If you fail to reimburse me I shall have no alternative but to issue a summons against you in the county court for recovery of the money without further reference to you.

Yours sincerely

Carpet shading: rejecting the retailer's and manufacturer's denials of liability

Dear

[Reference: make and name of carpet]

Thank you for your letter of **[date]** in which you passed on to me the manufacturer's denial of responsibility for carpet shading, on the basis of its being a phenomenon which can occur at random, rather than the result of a defect in manufacture. This argument is unacceptable.

It seems that shading is a known phenomenon which occurs in carpets of the type that I purchased, but you failed to warn me of this possibility at the time of purchase **[date]**. You are therefore in breach of contract under the amended Sale of Goods Act 1979, and I am legally entitled to redress. While reserving my rights I expect you to replace this carpet free of charge. I look forward to receiving your proposals for effecting this within the next 14 days.

Yours sincerely

Rejecting goods that are not delivered on time

Dear

[Reference: order number]

On **[date]** I placed the above order for **[item]** with you, for which I paid in advance. The **[item]** has still not been delivered.

Under the Sale of Goods Act 1979 you are required to deliver the **[item]** to me within a reasonable time. As **[period]** has elapsed since I placed the order, you have failed to fulfil this statutory requirement and are therefore in breach of contract.

I am now making time of the essence. If you do not send me the **[item]** within seven days, I will consider our contract at an end, as I am entitled to do in law, and will expect you to refund the full purchase price of **[£.....]** to me.

If you fail to deliver the **[item]** to me within seven days, I shall have no alternative but to issue a summons against you in the county court for recovery of the money without further reference to you.

Yours sincerely

Cancelling an order for late Christmas goods

Dear

[Reference: order number]

On **[date]** I ordered **[item]** from your Christmas Catalogue, enclosing full payment with my order. The **[item]** was not delivered until **[date after Christmas]**, and I was compelled to buy another **[item]** from a different supplier before Christmas at a cost of **[£.....]**.

You were obliged by the terms of our contract to supply me with the **[item]** in time for Christmas, and your failure to do so means that you are in breach of contract. I am therefore legally entitled to cancel the contract and to receive from you a refund of the **[£.....]**, being the full purchase price of **[£.....]** plus **[£.....]** postage and packing.

I look forward to receiving your cheque for **[£.....]** within 14 days. If you fail to reimburse me I shall have no alternative but to issue a summons against you in the county court for recovery of the money without further reference to you.

Yours sincerely

Rejecting defective mail-order goods

Dear

[Reference: order number]

I placed the above order for **[item]** on **[date]**. The **[item]** which I received on **[date]** showed serious defects **[describe]**.

Under the amended Sale of Goods Act 1979 you are obliged to supply goods that are of satisfactory quality. The fact that the **[item]** showed the above defects indicates that the goods supplied were not of satisfactory quality, and you are therefore in breach of contract. I am legally entitled to receive from you a full refund of the purchase price of **[£.....]** plus **[£.....]** paid towards postage and packing, making a total of **[£.....]**.

I look forward to receiving your cheque for **[£.....]** in the next 14 days. If you fail to reimburse me I shall have no alternative but to issue a summons against you in the county court for recovery of the money without further reference to you.

Yours sincerely

Rejecting mail-order goods that do not match their description

Dear

[Reference: order number]

I placed the above order on **[date]** for **[item]** described as **[quote]** on page **[.....]** of your catalogue. The **[item]** which I received on **[date]** differs from the description and illustrations in the catalogue in the following way **[describe differences]**.

Section 13 of the Sale of Goods Act 1979 requires you to supply goods that correspond with their description. As the **[item]** does not correspond with the description given in your catalogue, you are in breach of contract.

I am therefore legally entitled to receive from you a full refund of the **[£.....]** purchase price plus **[£.....]** postage and packing, making a total of **[£.....]**.

I look forward to receiving your cheque for **[£.....]** within the next 14 days. If you fail to reimburse me I shall have no alternative but to issue a summons against you in the county court for recovery of the money without further reference to you.

Yours sincerely

Rejecting mail-order goods damaged in transit

Dear

[Reference: order number]

On **[date]** I placed the above order for **[goods]** price
[£.....] as advertised in your **[.....]** catalogue. When
the **[goods]** were delivered on **[date]** I discovered the
following damage **[describe]**.

As you are a member of the Mail Order Trading
Association, you are governed by a code of practice
which states that you will either replace any goods
damaged in transit or refund the purchase price.

While reserving my rights, I would like you to supply a
replacement **[item]** within 14 days.

Yours sincerely

Chapter 2

Holidays and travel

WHEN your package holiday booking is accepted (usually by the issue of a confirmation invoice), a legally binding contract is made between you and the tour operator – the company that organises your holiday. The contract is *not* with the travel agent, and if things go wrong, your claim is against the tour operator. On the other hand, travel agents are under a legal obligation to do their job with reasonable skill and care, and you will have a claim if they do not.

Descriptions in the travel company's brochure of the hotel and the resort form part of your contract with the tour operator, and are therefore part of your legal entitlements. These descriptions must be factually accurate – this means that the hotel facilities specified in the brochure must exist as described, a 'quiet' hotel must be quiet, and the dates and times of flights must be correctly stated, too.

Along with the specific right to features described in the brochure, you also have rights implied into the contract by previous case law, to the effect that the accommodation provided will be of a standard of cleanliness and quality reasonably to be expected from the type and price of holiday booked, so you are in a position to claim if your holiday proves substandard in this regard. Complain on the spot and complete a dissatisfaction report.

Special requirements that you have communicated to the tour operator before making your booking, and which have been accepted by the tour operator are also part of your contract: so if you have specified a room with a sea view, or a ground-floor room for an elderly relative, for example, you are legally entitled to find them available when you arrive.

You can specifically ask the travel agent to act as agent on *your* behalf, instead of as agent of the tour operator, and to make a particular booking on particular terms. If the travel agent does not carry out your instructions when it claims it has, you will have a claim against the agent.

If, when you arrive at your destination, you find that the tour operator has failed to provide the holiday you booked, make sure you complain immediately to the tour operator's representative. If complaining at the time does not resolve your problem, write to the tour operator when you get home.

The Association of British Travel Agents (ABTA) is the main representative body for both travel agents and tour operators. It operates a bonding scheme to ensure holidaymakers do not lose their money when member companies go bust. It also operates a code of conduct which sets standards of service that are binding on members.

Accommodation

A tour operator's failure to provide you with the precise accommodation you booked is, on the face of it, a breach of contract on its part. Under an EU Directive, incorporated into English law by the Package Travel, Package Holidays and Package Tour Regulations 1992, and the ABTA code, operators must take due care to ensure that problems such as overbooking do not happen. You should also be informed by the operator as soon as the problem comes to light, so that you can cancel your holiday with that operator, or choose another one that it offers. However, many tour operators' brochures contain a term in the booking conditions denying liability for changes of plan caused by overbooking, which will probably prevent your claiming compensation so long as the alternative accommodation provided is of the same standard as that booked and is in a comparable part of the resort. But if the alternative offered is of a lower standard, or in a different resort, say, you will be entitled under the 1992 Package Travel Regulations to be repatriated and to compensation if you make a reasonable decision that the alternative is not suitable.

Working out your claim for compensation

The amount of compensation you could reasonably expect to receive depends to a large extent on the amount of enjoyment you were able to derive from your holiday. There are three basic components of holiday compensation:

- **Loss of value** – the difference between the value of the holiday you got and the one you paid for.
- **Loss of enjoyment** – something to compensate you for the disappointment and frustration of your holiday going wrong.
- **Out-of-pocket expenses** – the refund of any reasonable expenses you incurred as a result of the tour operator's breach of contract.

An example to work through

Below we show you how to calculate an imaginary claim: go through the same stages to work out your own claim. There are still subjective assessments involved, and there is no guarantee that the courts will reach the same conclusions if your claim has to go that far – but this at least gives you a starting point.

1. Take the total cost of the holiday as paid to the tour operator	Two people paying £400: total £800	A
2. Was the holiday a *complete disaster* as a result of the tour operator's breach of contract? If YES, go straight to stage 5	No, it was only the room which was unsatisfactory, and we were out on the beach most of the day	B
3. Subtract the cost of those parts of the holiday which were *not* affected by the problem, such as flights. (This is bound to be a 'guesstimate'.)	2 flights costing £130 each (£260) £800 – £260 = £540	C
4. What proportion of the problematic part of the holiday (i.e. the bit left after Stage 3) was ruined? This may involve a number of days which were totally spoiled, or a continuing problem which partially spoiled the whole of the holiday.	We were affected for the first five days of a two-week holiday, therefore 5/14 or 35% of the holiday was spoiled. 35% of £540 = £189	D
5. Did you incur any additional expenses as a direct result of the tour operator failing to provide the holiday you booked?	No, none	E
6. Put down an amount of compensation for loss of enjoyment, inconvenience, etc. (It is impossible to calculate this in any scientific way, but courts are allowing quite a lot of compensation for these.)	The unpleasantness of the room, plus the inconvenience of moving to the new one, entitles us to about £250 per person. £250 x 2 = £500	F
7. To get the total amount you should claim, add together amounts D + E + F.	£189 + £0 + £500 = £689 Say £700	

If the holiday was a complete disaster, add together A + E + F

If you do not achieve a satisfactory result, and your tour operator belongs to the ABTA (most do), you have the option of either going to court, perhaps using the small claims procedure in the county court, or using ABTA's arbitration scheme. You cannot do both, and you cannot go to court later if you are unhappy with the result of the arbitration.

The arbitration scheme is run for ABTA by the Chartered Institute of Arbitrators to resolve disputes between member tour operators and customers. Consumers' Association does not normally recommend arbitration, because it works on a documents-only basis – which means that you have to match the written skills of the tour operator's professional advisers. An oral account of your troubles in court is likely to have a greater impact in your favour. It is up to you, however, to decide which is best for you – going to court or using the arbitration scheme.

Problems with airlines

Package holidays and charters

If your tour operator changes your flight, look at the booking conditions in the brochure: unless the conditions allow such changes, the tour operator is not entitled to do this. Unfortunately, most booking conditions, and the ABTA code, *do* allow minor changes to flight times. However, you should be given a full refund, or some kind of compensation, if you decide to cancel when the operator makes a major change. In this instance, major and minor are not precisely defined and depend on the circumstances of each case.

Scheduled flights

Under the Warsaw Convention, incorporated into English law by the Carriage by Air and Road Act 1979, airlines are obliged to compensate you if they fail to get you to your destination within a reasonable time of your scheduled arrival. On a long-haul flight, a 'reasonable' time is usually considered to be about six hours. The strength of your claim depends on what causes the delay. If it is a factor outside the airline's control – bad weather, for example – you do not stand much chance of recompense. But if your delay is a result of overbooking, or any other cause within the airline's control, you do have a valid claim and it is worth persisting.

There is also a European Union Regulation covering overbooking on scheduled flights from European destinations. If you turn up at an airport within the European Union and are denied boarding because the flight you have booked is already full, you will be entitled to a full refund of the unused ticket, or a seat on the next available flight of your choice. The airline must also offer you immediate cash compensation: you are currently entitled to £120 for flights of up to 3,500 kilometres, and £240 for longer flights. These amounts are halved if the airline can get you to your final destination within two hours (or four hours for flights over 3,500 km) of your original scheduled arrival. You must also be given a free telephone call to your destination, meals throughout the delay and overnight accommodation if it is necessary.

Problems with luggage

If your luggage is lost, damaged or even delayed on an international flight, you may have a claim against the airline for compensation. The Warsaw Convention allows you to claim a maximum sum, currently £13.63, per kilogram of checked-in baggage. This limitation applies whether your case is full of expensive designer clothes or old T-shirts and jeans. If your luggage is returned to you damaged, you must make your complaint to the airline within seven days of getting it back.

Informing a travel agent of specific holiday requirements

Dear

[Reference: booking number]

I wish to book a holiday **[dates, location, price]** as advertised by **[operator]** on page **[.....]** of its current brochure. I enclose the appropriate booking form, duly completed.

Please note that I have the following special needs **[describe]** and that I have selected this particular holiday because it offers **[features advertised in brochure]**.

Please ensure that I am booked into accommodation that fits the above requirements, and confirm in writing that this has been done and that the tour operator is aware of my special needs.

I look forward to hearing from you.

Yours sincerely

Complaining to a travel agent about specific holiday requirements not met

Dear

[Reference: booking number]

I wish to complain about my recent holiday, **[operator, dates, location, price]**.

On **[date]** I advised you in writing that I required the following specific features **[describe]**. Your letter of **[date]** confirmed that these facilities would be provided and that they were included in the holiday you booked on my behalf. However, none was provided **[expand if necessary]**.

You were under a legal contractual obligation to book a holiday in accordance with my specific instructions, and to advise me if that could not be done. As you failed to fulfil my requirements, I hold you fully liable for the disappointment I suffered.

Please let me know within 14 days how you propose to resolve this matter.

Yours sincerely

Complaining to a tour operator about overbooking

Dear

[Reference: booking number]

I booked the above holiday with you **[dates, location, hotel, price]**.

When I arrived I was told that the above hotel was fully booked and that alternative accommodation was provided at **[hotel, other details]**. I complained immediately to your representative but the matter was not resolved to my satisfaction.

It was an express term of the contract between us that I would stay at the **[initial hotel]**. Your failure to provide accommodation at that hotel, or at a hotel of comparable standard in the same resort, constitutes a breach of that contract. The change of accommodation **[and venue, if appropriate]** ruined my holiday and caused considerable disappointment and inconvenience.

I am entitled to compensation for the consequences of your breach of contract. As I experienced **[problem]**, I look to you to pay me **[£.....]** in compensation, calculated on the basis of **[details of calculation]**.

I look forward to receiving your cheque within the next 14 days. If you fail to reimburse me I shall have no alternative but to issue a summons against you in the county court for recovery of the money without further reference to you.

Yours sincerely

Complaining to a tour operator about substandard accommodation

Dear

[Reference: booking number]

I have just returned from the above holiday, which according to your brochure should have comprised **[details]**.

The hotel's facilities, for which I booked and paid, on the understanding that they were as described in your brochure, constituted the terms of my contract with you. It was implied in these terms that the accommodation provided would be of a standard of cleanliness and quality reasonably to be expected for this type and price of holiday.

The accommodation was unsatisfactory in the following ways **[details]**. When I asked to be moved to satisfactory accommodation, I was told by your representative that this was not possible; nor were the problems rectified. You are therefore in breach of contract, and I am legally entitled to receive compensation from you. I am in consequence claiming the sum of **[£.....]**.

If within 14 days you have not made a reasonable offer of compensation, I shall have no alternative but to sue you in the county court.

Yours sincerely

Complaining to a tour operator about misleading descriptions of accommodation

Dear

[Reference; booking number]

I have just returned from the above holiday **[dates, location, hotel etc.]** as described on **[page .....]** of your **[.....]** brochure.

The hotel was misleadingly described. It purported to be **[describe from brochure]** but I experienced the following problems **[describe]**. My complaints to the hotel management and to your representative were fruitless. Your failure to mention **[circumstances]** in the brochure description is misleading, and in law amounts to a misrepresentation. The brochure's description was embodied in our contract and as the description was inaccurate, you are also in breach of contract.

I am legally entitled to receive compensation from you for the disappointment and loss of enjoyment suffered, and for the additional costs incurred. As a result of the problems described above, I incurred the following expenses **[list]**.

I look to you to compensate me with **[£.....]**.

If within 14 days you have not made a reasonable offer of compensation, I shall have no alternative but to sue you in the county court.

Yours sincerely

Rejecting a tour operator's unacceptable offer of compensation

Dear

[Reference: booking number]

Thank you for your letter of **[date]**.

Your offer of **[£.....]** in response to my letter of **[date]** claiming **[£.....]** compensation is unacceptable.

I am therefore writing to inform you that, unless I receive your satisfactory proposals for settlement of my outstanding claim within 14 days of the date of this letter, I intend to issue a summons against you in the county court without further reference to you.

Yours sincerely

Complaining to an airline about flight delays

Dear

[Reference: flight number]

I am writing to you in connection with the above flight, which I took on **[date]**.

The flight was supposed to depart from **[departure airport]** at **[time]**, but did not take off until **[time]** arriving at **[destination]** at **[time]**. When I complained to your staff, I was told that the delay was due to **[reason]**.

It was a term of the contract between us that you get me to my destination within a reasonable time of the scheduled time of arrival. As you failed to do so, you are in breach of contract. Since the delay was due to circumstances within your control, I am entitled to receive compensation from you for the considerable inconvenience caused to me by the delay.

I look forward to receiving a reasonable offer of compensation from you within the next 14 days.

Yours sincerely

Complaining to an airline about lost luggage

Dear

[Reference: flight number]

On **[date]** I was a passenger on the above flight.

My luggage, which was checked in at **[departure airport]**, never arrived at **[destination]**. The loss was reported to your company staff on arrival and the appropriate luggage report form was completed. I have not heard from you since.

Under the terms of the Warsaw Convention I am entitled to receive compensation from you for my lost luggage. The items in question **[describe]** weighed **[amount]**. I therefore calculate my loss as **[£.....]**.

I look forward to receiving a reasonable offer of compensation from you within the next 14 days.

Yours sincerely

Rejecting an airline's unacceptable offer of compensation for lost luggage

Dear

[Reference: flight number]

Further to your letter of **[date]** in which you offered **[£.....]** in settlement of my claim of **[date]**, I wish to inform you that your offer is unacceptable.

I look forward to receiving your cheque for **[£.....]** in settlement of my claim within 14 days. If you fail to reimburse me I shall have no alternative but to issue a summons against you in the county court without further reference to you.

Yours sincerely

Chapter 3

Hotels and restaurants

WHEN you book hotel accommodation or eat out in a pub, café or restaurant, you enter into a contract with the provider of the service. If a dispute arises between you and the service-provider, the contract defines the legal status of both parties and gives you rights.

Many of the rights mentioned in this chapter arise from the common law rather than specific pieces of legislation. However, the Supply of Goods and Services Act 1982 ensures that you should receive a reasonable standard of accommodation and service in England, Wales and Northern Ireland (common law in Scotland).

Criminal laws – laws enforced by public authorities – also affect your dealings with hotels and restaurants. The most important criminal laws in this respect are:

- **The Food Safety Act 1990,** covering hygiene in places where the public eats.
- **The Trade Descriptions Act 1968,** which ensures that statements in menus and other promotional literature are accurate.
- **The Consumer Protection Act 1987,** which prevents misleading price indications. A code of practice introduced under the Act says, for example, that hotels and restaurants should include any compulsory service charge within the price of each item (rather than adding a percentage to the total bill), but only where this is 'practicable'.

Claiming your rights

If you have a problem, try to sort out the matter on the spot. Ask to speak to the manager, explain what the problem is and how you wish it to be rectified – by being given a substitute dish, for example.

If you are not able to come to an agreement with the manager, you are entitled to deduct a suitable amount from the bill. Work out the extent to which you feel your stay or meal was spoiled; for example, if your cheesecake was frozen solid, you could deduct the charge for this. If circumstances do not permit this course of action, pay the entire bill, making clear that you are paying under protest. Paying the bill under protest keeps your options open to claim your legal rights later.

If you are in any doubt as to your rights, get advice from a Citizens Advice Bureau, Law Centre or Consumer Advice Centre. The Trading Standards or Consumer Protection department of your local authority may also be able to help. If you go to a solicitor, check first how much it is likely to cost you (see page 193).

When you have found out your legal position, write to the proprietor or manager. Remind him or her of the problem, and what you want done to resolve it.

A lost booking

When you book a room or table in advance, you make a contract with the hotel or restaurant obliging it to provide you with what you have booked for the requisite number of people at the time you specified. If it does not do so, there is a breach of contract and you can claim a reasonable sum to cover any expenses you incur as a result, such as travel costs. You can also claim a reasonable sum to compensate you for any disappointment and inconvenience suffered. The amount you can claim will depend on the importance to you of staying or eating at that particular place and the trouble involved in making other arrangements. If the complaint concerns a booking for a special occasion, and the establishment had been specifically chosen to celebrate the event, the amount of compensation that the customer can claim is substantial.

Unsatisfactory food

The descriptions of food and wine on the menu form part of your contract with the establishment – 'home-made soup', for example, must be home-made, not canned or from a packet. In addition, under the Supply of Goods and Services Act 1982 (common law in Scotland), kitchens are obliged to prepare food with reasonable skill and care: frozen food must be properly defrosted, for example, and cooked food must not be raw. If you think that the food which is served to you does not correspond to its description on the menu, or has not been prepared with reasonable skill and care, do not continue eating it. Complain immediately and ask for something else.

If you are not able to have the problem rectified to your satisfaction, you can deduct what you think is a fair and reasonable sum from the bill. Alternatively, you can pay under protest and claim compensation later.

Poor service

If a service charge is automatically added to the bill, this must be clearly indicated both outside the building and immediately inside its door. You then have to pay the charge unless the service was not of a reasonable standard for that type of establishment, in which case you can refuse to pay all or part of the service charge. If, for example, a member of staff has spilled food or drink on you, the service would not have been reasonable and you would not have to pay a service charge. You could also claim the cost of cleaning the clothes damaged by the spillage. The reasonableness of the service is dictated by the type of place you are in and the price you are asked to pay for the meal and service. Service which might be thought acceptable in a roadside café would not be reasonable in the grill-room of a four star hotel.

If, on the other hand, a service charge is not indicated, you do not have to pay – it is up to you whether or not to tip, and if so, by how much.

Food poisoning

If you think that the food you ate made you ill, tell your doctor immediately. Proving who is responsible may be difficult, but you would have a stronger case if more than one person was affected. If you can prove that the kitchen caused your illness, you can claim compensation for your pain, suffering and any loss of earnings and other expenses you incur as a result. In particularly serious cases, get advice from a solicitor on how much to claim.

You should also inform your local Environmental Health Department. An Environmental Health Officer can investigate the incident and may decide to prosecute; under the Food Safety Act 1990 it is a criminal offence for a business to serve food which is unfit for human consumption.

Stolen goods

Hoteliers owe you a legal duty to take care of your property while it is in their hotel. They are liable to you for any loss or damage to your goods, provided you are not to blame (by leaving expensive jewellery next to an open window, for example). However, the Hotel Proprietors Act 1956 allows hotel owners to limit their liability to £50 per item or £100 in total if they display a notice to this effect at reception. They cannot rely on this limit, though, if the negligence of their staff caused the loss, although you will have to prove this.

Complaining to a restaurant about a booking that was not kept

Dear

On **[date]** I booked a table for **[.....]** people at your restaurant for **[time, day, date]**. When making the booking, I made it clear that it was for **[details of special occasion]**.

When we arrived at your restaurant as per the booking, we discovered **[problem: details]**. On this special occasion, I was not prepared to wait **[time]** for a table and had no choice but to make alternative arrangements.

Your failure to provide the table booked in advance amounts to a breach of contract, which led in this case to considerable disappointment, distress and loss of enjoyment **[reason why]**. You are in breach of contract, and I am entitled to receive compensation from you for expenses incurred, as well as a reasonable sum to compensate for the disappointment and inconvenience suffered.

I therefore claim **[£.....]** compensation and look forward to receiving your cheque for that amount within 14 days. If you fail to reimburse me I shall have no alternative but to issue a summons against you in the county court for recovery of the money without further reference to you.

Yours sincerely

Complaining to a restaurant about an unsatisfactory meal

Dear

On **[day, date]**, my party of **[number]** ate **[meal]** at your restaurant. Our meal was unsatisfactory in the following ways: **[describe item by item]**.

I complained immediately, but after the meal I was presented with a bill for **[£.....]** which included the cost of uneaten dishes. I wished to deduct the cost of uneaten dishes as I am entitled to do in law, but was not permitted to do so **[describe circumstances]**. As I had no option but to pay the bill in full, I did so on the express understanding that I was paying under protest and would claim compensation from you later.

It was a term of my contract with you that the food would be as described on your menu, and an implied term of the contract that the standard of food and service be reasonable. You are therefore in breach of contract, and I am entitled to receive compensation for both your breach of contract and the consequences thereof. I was unable to derive any real benefit or pleasure from the meal, so I expect you to pay me **[£..... full price of meal]** in compensation.

I look forward to receiving your cheque for that amount within the next 14 days. If you fail to reimburse me I shall have no alternative but to issue a summons against you in the county court for recovery of the money without further reference to you.

Yours sincerely

Complaining to a restaurant about unacceptable service

Dear

At **[time]** on **[day, date]** my party of **[number]** ate **[meal]** in your restaurant. The service we received was unsatisfactory in a number of ways **[describe]** and we had **[wine, sauce etc.]** spilt on our clothes. The cost of rectifying the damage to our clothes was **[£.....]** and in law I am entitled to claim that amount from you as compensation.

I look forward to receiving your cheque for that amount within the next 14 days. If you fail to reimburse me I shall have no alternative but to issue a summons against you in the county court for recovery of the money without further reference to you.

Yours sincerely

Complaining to a restaurant about food poisoning

Dear

At **[time]** on **[day, date]** my party of **[number]** ate **[meal]** at your restaurant. I am writing to let you know that members of my party became seriously ill with food poisoning following the meal.

I have been advised by my GP that the food poisoning almost certainly resulted from the food which had been eaten at your restaurant. This is because **[details]**.

You are legally obliged to serve food which is fit for human consumption under the terms of the contract between restaurant and consumer. Your failure to do so indicates that you are in breach of contract. As a result, we are legally entitled to receive compensation from you for our pain and suffering, loss of earnings and out-of-pocket expenses.

We are taking legal advice on the extent of our claim and will be in touch with you shortly to advise you of the figure.

I have also contacted the Environmental Health Department, which will be investigating the matter.

Yours sincerely

Complaining to a hotel about a substandard room

Dear

On **[date]** I stayed at your hotel for **[number]** night(s) in room **[number]**.

As I mentioned to your receptionist at the time, the accommodation was unsatisfactory in the following ways: **[describe]**. When I asked to be moved to another room, I was told that this was not possible; nor were the problems rectified.

It was an implied term of our contract that the accommodation provided would be of a standard of cleanliness and quality reasonably to be expected from this type and price of hotel. The fact that the accommodation was not of a reasonable standard as required by the Supply of Goods and Services Act 1982 shows that you are in breach of contract.

I am therefore legally entitled to receive compensation from you. In consequence I am claiming the sum of [£.....].

If within 14 days you have not offered compensation, I shall have no alternative but to sue you in the county court.

Yours sincerely

Complaining to a hotel about misdescribed facilities

Dear

On **[date]** I stayed at your hotel for **[number]** night(s) in room **[number]**.

As I mentioned to your receptionist at the time, the facilities available at your hotel were misleadingly described in the brochure provided by you before I booked my stay. You hotel purported to have the following facilities: **[describe from brochure]**. However, I experienced the following problems **[describe]**. My complaints to **[member of staff]** were fruitless. Your failure accurately to describe the facilities available at your hotel and your failure to mention **[circumstances]** in the brochure description is misleading and amounts to a misrepresentation.

The brochure's description of your hotel and the facilities was embodied in our contract. As the description was inaccurate, you are also in breach of contract.

I am legally entitled to receive compensation from you for the disappointment and loss of enjoyment suffered. In consequence, I am claiming the sum of [£.....].

If within 14 days you have not made a reasonable offer of compensation, I shall have no alternative but to sue you in the county court.

Yours sincerely

Complaining to a hotel about stolen items

Dear

On **[date]** I stayed at your hotel for **[number]** night(s) in room **[number]**.

While staying at your hotel a theft occurred in my room on **[date]**. The thief got into my room because one of your staff failed to lock the door after cleaning the room. I reported the loss to your staff at the time. However, I have not heard from you since.

You were under a legal duty to look after my property while it was on your premises. The fact that the thief entered my room because your cleaner failed to lock the door clearly shows that you were negligent. Because of your negligence I have lost the following item(s): **[describe]**. I calculate my loss as **[£.....]**.

I am legally entitled to be reimbursed in full for the loss of my property. I therefore claim the sum of **[£.....]** from you.

If within 14 days you have not offered compensation, I shall have no alternative but to sue you in the county court.

Yours sincerely

Chapter 4

Buying cars

Buying a new car

When you buy a new car from a dealer, you are covered by the Sale of Goods Act 1979 (as amended by the Sale and Supply of Goods Act 1994). This means that the car must fit its description, be of satisfactory quality and (if you advise the retailer that the car is for a special purpose, such as rallying) be fit for its purpose. If the car does not meet these requirements, you have a claim against the dealer. If your car is defective, for example, you are legally entitled to ask the dealer to collect it from you and refund the full purchase price to you.

If you decide to reject the car and claim a full refund of the purchase price, you must act as soon as possible: you have only a reasonable time period following purchase of the vehicle to reject it and get your money back. If you do not act promptly, and your claim is disputed, a court might subsequently decide that you had had the car too long to reject it, and that the dealer was no longer under an obligation to give you a full refund. So it is essential to check a vehicle thoroughly when you take possession of it. If it is too late for you to reject the car, you are still legally entitled to compensation, which is usually the cost of repair.

Guarantees and warranties offer useful cover. The right kind of guarantee can add to the appeal of buying a specific car. Study the guarantee's wording carefully. But remember, whatever the terms of the scheme are, your rights under the amended Sale of Goods Act 1979 still stand.

Buying a second-hand car

When you buy a second-hand car from a dealer, you have the same rights under the amended Sale of Goods Act 1979 as if the car were new. In other words it should fit its description, be of satisfactory quality and reasonably fit for its purpose.

You cannot expect a second-hand car to be in the same condition as a new car, but you are entitled to expect it to be roadworthy. The quality and condition of the car to which you are legally entitled will depend very much on the price you pay for it, its appearance, and any descriptions of it used to sell it to you – 'in perfect running condition', for instance.

When you are buying a second-hand car, you should examine and test it before committing yourself. If the examination reveals a defect, or if the dealer tells you about a specific defect before you buy, the dealer is not responsible for those particular defects affecting its performance after purchase.

If a defect which was not discovered when you examined the car comes to light after you have bought it, and you tell the dealer immediately, you may be entitled to reject the car and get your money back. Remember, you only have a reasonable time in which to reject faulty goods, and this can be as short as a couple of weeks. After that your claim is for compensation, which is calculated as the difference between what you paid for the car and its market value, taking into account the defects. This is usually taken as the cost of repairs.

Many dealers also offer customers the opportunity of buying an 'extended warranty' for second-hand cars. This is basically a type of insurance against mechanical breakdown for a certain period of time or mileage and can be a useful form of cover in addition to your rights under the Sale of Goods Act 1979.

Clocking

If the car you bought had a false odometer reading when you purchased it, and there was no indication (a sticker, for example) warning you that the odometer may have been wrong, you will have a claim under the Sale of Goods Act 1979 for misdescription, and also under the Misrepresentation Act 1967 for misrepresentation.

If the car does not match its description (including its mileage), the seller may be breaking the Trade Descriptions Act 1968. This says that it is a criminal offence for dealers to make false statements about the cars they sell. The Act is enforced by local Trading Standards Departments. Since it is a criminal law, the Act cannot help you directly if you want to make a claim for compensation, but it is worth threatening to report the matter to the local Trading Standards Department. This may lead to a quick settlement of your claim.

How to claim

Whatever the problem with your car, contact the dealer about it immediately. Explain the problem and try to reach some sort of compromise. If your problem is not resolved, write a letter of complaint to the manager or owner of the garage, explaining what is wrong and what you want done about it.

Some garages claim that it is not their responsibility to sort out problems with faulty vehicles, and that the responsibility lies with the manufacturer. Do not be fobbed off. Remember that your contract is with the retailer who sold you the goods and that this contract gives you rights under the amended Sale of Goods Act 1979. So if your claim is rejected initially, or your first letter goes unanswered, be persistent. Remind the dealer of his legal obligations under the amended Sale of Goods Act.

The law does not require you to take the car back to the dealer; the dealer can be instructed to collect it from you. You should therefore arrange this once you have received his cheque. It may be that the only response to your letters of complaint will be an offer to repair the car under warranty. If this happens, consider this option carefully. The only alternative to a free repair would be for you to sue for the refund of your money. Since a substantial sum may be at stake, you should take legal advice from a solicitor.

Many garages are members of one of the trade associations which adhere to the motor industry code of practice. If the dealer who sold you the car is a member and you are having difficulty achieving your aims, tell the association about your complaint as soon as possible. They may be able to help resolve the problem (see

Addresses at the back of this book). If writing to one of these organisations does not resolve the problem to your satisfaction, you have the choice of going to court (see Chapter 17) or taking your claim to arbitration. The trade associations run their own schemes in conjunction with the Chartered Institute of Arbitrators. Your case will be read by an independent arbitrator who will study your evidence and the evidence of the dealer and come to a decision, but if you are unhappy with the result you will not be able to go to court later.

Asking a dealer for a free repair to a new car

Dear

[Reference: registration number of vehicle]

On **[date]** I bought the above vehicle **[make, model, engine capacity]** from you. On **[date]** it developed serious defects **[describe]**.

Section 14 of the amended Sale of Goods Act 1979 requires you to supply goods of satisfactory quality. The fact that the vehicle developed the **[defects]** shows that it was faulty at the time of purchase. It was therefore not of satisfactory quality and you are consequently in breach of contract.

In these circumstances, I am legally entitled to financial compensation. However, while fully reserving my rights under the amended Sale of Goods Act, I am prepared to give you an opportunity to repair the **[defects]** without any charge to me. Please let me know what arrangements you can make to undertake this work speedily.

I look forward to receiving your proposals for reparation within the next 14 days.

Yours sincerely

NOTE
If you ask for a repair, always reserve your amended Sale of Goods Act rights while doing so; then, if the retailer does not carry out a free repair or if the repair is faulty, you can still claim compensation.

Rejecting a dealer's denial of liability

Dear

[Reference: registration number of vehicle]

Thank you for your letter of **[date]** in which you deny responsibility for the defects in the above vehicle **[make, model, engine capacity]** which I described in my letter of **[date]**.

I must remind you that my claim against you is based on the amended Sale of Goods Act 1979. As I pointed out in my previous letter, Section 14 of the Act requires the retailer, *not* the manufacturer, to supply goods which are of satisfactory quality and reasonably fit for their purpose. Your failure to supply goods of the requisite quality means that I have a claim against you for breach of contract. This claim is not affected by any rights I may have under the guarantee offered by the manufacturer.

I trust that this clarifies the situation and I therefore expect you to arrange for a free repair to the vehicle within the next 14 days.

Yours sincerely

Rejecting a second-hand car bought from a dealer

Dear

[Reference: registration number of vehicle]

On **[date]** I purchased and took delivery of the above vehicle **[make, model, engine capacity]** from you. On **[date]** I discovered that it had serious defects **[describe]**. An independent examination by **[garage]** revealed that the vehicle was unfit to drive.

Section 14 of the amended Sale of Goods Act 1979 requires dealers to supply goods of satisfactory quality. The results of the inspection clearly show that the vehicle was unroadworthy. You are therefore in breach of contract. Furthermore, I was influenced in my decision to purchase the car by the wording of your advertisement **[where displayed]**, describing it as **[quote]**, which gave me to believe that the vehicle was in good running order. The fact that it was not means that you are in breach of the Sale of Goods Act 1979 in misdescribing the vehicle, and furthermore that you are liable for misrepresentation under the Misrepresentation Act 1967.

I am therefore legally entitled to reject the vehicle and to be reimbursed for its full purchase price of **[£.....]**. I look forward to receiving your cheque for this sum within 14 days. If you fail to reimburse me I shall have no alternative but to issue a summons against you in the county court for recovery of the money without further reference to you.

Yours sincerely   NOTE See page 14 for Scotland/N. Ireland.

Rejecting a second-hand car which has been 'clocked'

Dear

[Reference: registration number of vehicle]

On **[date]** I bought the above vehicle **[make, model, engine capacity]** from you. The car had **[.....]** miles on the odometer. I have since ascertained from previous sales documents relating to the car that the mileage is substantially greater than this, which suggests that the odometer has been altered.

The Sale of Goods Act 1979 provides that goods must comply with their description. As it was an implied term of my contract with you that the car's mileage was **[.....]**, the fact that the true mileage is **[.....]** means that you are in breach of contract. I also have a claim against you for misrepresentation under the Misrepresentation Act 1967.

I am exercising my legal right to reject the car and to receive from you the full purchase price of **[£.....]**.

Furthermore, you are in breach of the Trade Descriptions Act 1968 which makes it a criminal offence to give false descriptions and statements about goods. I shall be sending details of this matter to the Trading Standards Department in due course.

I look forward to hearing from you by return of post.

Yours sincerely

Chapter 5

Garage servicing

IF YOU have a complaint about the service you have received from a garage – poor repair work or overcharging, say – take it up with the garage straight away, explaining clearly why you are not satisfied. It may be a question of a misunderstanding that the garage can easily put right. If your problem is not resolved, write a letter of complaint to the manager or owner of the garage, explaining what is wrong and what you want done to rectify it. You should always give the garage an opportunity to put faulty work right, because you are under a legal duty to keep your claim as small as is reasonably possible.

If the garage is unwilling or unable to resolve the problem, and it belongs to a trade association (it is advisable to check this before getting your car serviced), write asking the association to intervene (see Addresses at the back of this book).

The trade associations run their own schemes in conjunction with the Chartered Institute of Arbitrators (see Addresses at the back of this book). If you do take your case to arbitration, you cannot go to court later if you are unhappy with the result.

A poor service or repair

If you ask a garage to service or repair your car and it is damaged in the process, or fails to function for a reasonable time after the repair because the work has not been carried out properly, then the garage is in breach of contract. You are entitled to claim compensation for any loss or damage arising from this breach, which usually means the cost of getting the damage repaired. However, you should also be compensated for any expenses you incur which were reasonably foreseeable by both you and the garage at the time the contract was made, such as the cost of alternative means of transport while your car was off the road. But you must do what you can to ensure that your claim is kept to a minimum. If you cannot show that you have minimised your loss in this way, you run the risk of not being able to recover all your costs if the matter eventually goes to court.

Overcharging

When you ask a garage to repair or service your car, you are obliged to pay only for work you have authorised. So make sure you know exactly what you have agreed to before allowing the garage to carry out any work, preferably by putting it in writing. If the price is not agreed beforehand, the law says that you are obliged to pay a reasonable price for the work. There are no hard and fast rules about what this is: it depends on the type of repair or service that was undertaken. If you feel that the price you have been charged is too high, you will have to demonstrate that the price is unreasonable, so get evidence in the form of quotations for the same work from other garages, or from a motoring organisation if you belong to one. A useful tip is to ask the initial garage to give you an estimate as soon as the problem has been diagnosed.

If you are forced to pay as a condition for recovering your car, you should make it clear, preferably in writing, that you are paying under protest. This keeps your rights open to seek redress later.

Damage to a vehicle while it is in the garage's possession

When you take your car into a garage for repairs, the garage is legally obliged to take reasonable care of it. If your car is damaged while in the possession of the garage – on the garage forecourt or in a car wash, for example – the garage is responsible, under the law of bailment, for that damage unless it can prove that the damage was caused through no fault on its part.

Garages may attempt to restrict your legal rights by displaying notices denying responsibility for any loss or damage to vehicles left in their possession. Under the Unfair Contract Terms Act 1977 and the Unfair Terms in Consumer Contracts Regulations 1994, notices or conditions in contracts which seek to exclude or restrict liability for loss or damage to property will be upheld *only* if it can proved that they are fair and reasonable in all the circumstances. It is very unlikely that a court would uphold a garage's claim to be exempt from all responsibility for loss and damage to vehicles in its possession, whatever the cause.

Complaining about the unsatisfactory servicing of a vehicle

Dear

[Reference: registration number of vehicle]

On **[date]** I asked you to service the above vehicle **[make, model, engine capacity]**. When I collected the vehicle from you on **[date]**, I was told that you had carried out a 'full service', had diagnosed **[particular faults: specify]** and had repaired the vehicle accordingly **[specify if necessary]**. The bill for this work was **[£.....]**.

On **[date]**, **[.....]** days after the service, the vehicle developed serious faults **[describe in detail]**, rendering the vehicle unfit to drive and costing **[£.....]** to rectify. A copy of the receipt for that work is enclosed.

You were under a legal obligation to carry out the work on my **[vehicle]** with reasonable skill and care, using parts of satisfactory quality and fit for their purpose, as laid down by the Supply of Goods and Services Act 1982.

The above faults indicate that you failed to do so, and I am therefore legally entitled to receive compensation from you for breach of contract. I look forward to receiving your cheque for **[£.....]**, representing **[expenses incurred]**, within the next 14 days. If you fail to reimburse me I shall have no alternative but to issue a summons against you in the county court for recovery of the money without further reference to you.

Yours sincerely

enc.

Disputing a garage's excessive charge for vehicle servicing

Dear

[Reference: registration number of vehicle]

On **[date]** I asked your service manager to repair the above vehicle as follows: **[describe]**. I was told that this work would cost **[£.....]** but on collecting the vehicle, I was charged **[£.....]**.

Since we did not agree a fixed price for this work, I am legally obliged to pay only a reasonable price for the work. To ascertain a reasonable price, I asked two other garages, **[names]**, to estimate the cost of the work. They quoted **[£.....]** and **[£.....]**, respectively **[£.....]** and **[£.....]** less than your final bill of **[£.....]**. It is therefore clear that your final bill is unreasonable.

In accordance with my legal rights I am prepared to pay only the sum of **[£.....]**, based on your original estimate and the two subsequent quotations obtained elsewhere, in full and final settlement.

Yours sincerely

Complaining to a garage about damage to a vehicle while in its possession

Dear

[Reference: registration number of vehicle]

On **[date]** I took the above vehicle **[make, model, engine capacity]** into your garage for a full service. While in your possession, it was damaged as follows: **[describe]**.

You were under a legal duty to take care of my car while it was in your possession. Furthermore, the Supply of Goods and Services Act 1982 requires you to use reasonable care and skill while carrying out work. The fact that the **[vehicle]** was damaged while in your possession is evidence that you failed to take reasonable care of it.

I look forward to receiving, within the next 14 days, your written proposal to effect a satisfactory repair to the vehicle, at no cost to me. If you fail to respond in that time, I shall exercise my common law right to employ another garage to carry out the work and look to you to bear the cost. Any attempt to resist paying such a bill would leave me with no alternative but to issue a summons against you in the county court for recovery of the money without further reference to you.

Yours sincerely

Chapter 6

Property

Problems with your new house

The purchase of houses is covered by the legal principle of *caveat emptor*, or 'let the buyer beware': the onus is on the buyer to ascertain the quality and condition of a property before proceeding with a purchase. There are no implied terms in the contract of sale that the property is free from defects, and as a result the purchaser has little comeback against the seller if defects are found after purchase. As purchaser, you do not have the same rights as you have with the sale of goods, such as cars and washing machines, because the law pertaining to the sale of houses does not include an implied term that the property will be of satisfactory quality.

Fortunately, almost all new homes are covered by a warranty scheme which guarantees that they are built to certain standards and that, if they are not, problems will be put right either by the builder, or, where the builder will not co-operate, by the warranty firm. It is very unlikely that you would be able to borrow money for a new home that does not have a warranty.

Until recently there was one housing warranty for new homes – the National House Building Council (NHBC) Buildmark scheme. Through the scheme the NHBC sets minimum standards of workmanship which builders of new properties must achieve, inspects a builder's homes and guarantees them for buyers. It covers most of the market, but another guarantee scheme, called Foundation 15, run by Zurich Insurance, also offers similar protection to Buildmark.

Under the NHBC Buildmark guarantee scheme, during the first two years after purchase the builder of the property undertakes to put right any defects which result from the failure to comply with the NHBC's minimum standards of workmanship. For the next eight years, the NHBC undertakes to make good any major defects in the load-bearing structure. If there is a disagreement between the purchaser and the builder, the NHBC may be asked to intervene.

Foundation 15 offers similar cover for the first two years, but its cover relating to structural repair lasts a further 13 years, giving a total of 15 years' warranty.

Taking a dispute over a new property to the NHBC

If a dispute is not resolved by negotiation between the purchaser of the new home and the builder, the purchaser can ask the NHBC either to conciliate or to arrange an arbitration hearing (see Addresses at the back of this book).

Conciliation is informal and free of charge. An NHBC official will arrange to inspect the property in the presence of the purchaser and the builder. He will decide what work has to be done by the builder and the date by which it must be completed. The builder should then carry out the work recommended by the NHBC official. The purchaser and the builder have to agree to conciliation. If either side does not, the purchaser has no option but arbitration. Similarly, if he is not happy with the NHBC inspector's report, or if the builder fails to carry out the work recommended in the report, the purchaser may apply for arbitration.

Arbitration is a much more formal procedure than conciliation and is governed by the Arbitration Act 1996; arbitration is independent of the NHBC, the role of which is limited to administering the relevant application documents when you ask for an arbitration hearing. The arbitrator who hears the case is appointed from the Chartered Institute of Arbitrators by its president, who is himself unconnected with the NHBC.

There is no fixed scale of fees – liability to pay costs is decided by the arbitrator. Generally, if the purchaser wins, the builder will pay the costs, but arbitration does need serious consideration, since the cost to the purchaser could be considerable if he loses – he may have to pay the builder's costs, too. Furthermore, the arbitrator's decision is final, and neither party can go to court later if he is unhappy with the decision.

Estate agents

Estate agents are usually instructed by and act on behalf of sellers of properties. Estate agents' work is regulated by the Estate Agents Act 1979 and regulations and orders made under the Act. The purpose of these laws is to make sure that estate agents act in the best interests of their clients and that both buyers and sellers of property are treated honestly, fairly and promptly. The Director General of Fair Trading is responsible for the working and enforcement of the law. Trading standards departments and, in Northern Ireland, the Department of Economic Development are also enforcement authorities (see Addresses at the back of the book). Also, the Property Misdescriptions Act 1991 states that property misdescriptions are unlawful.

If you instruct an estate agent to sell your home, your legal position is governed by the law of contract – it is up to the seller to specify the services required when appointing the estate agent, and to make sure that the agent agrees to perform them. The seller also has rights under the Supply of Goods and Services Act 1982 (common law in Scotland), which states that the estate agent must perform the service with reasonable skill and care. In addition, under the common law of agency, the estate agent is obliged always to act in the best interests of the client. Unfortunately, there are no hard and fast rules about what precisely estate agents have to do to find a purchaser, so when choosing an estate agent you should contact several offices to find out exactly what services are offered.

The estate agent's commission is normally a percentage of the price at which the property is sold. Broadly, the range is likely to be within 1 to 2.5 per cent. Check what is included in the price – photographs, a 'For Sale' board and advertisements in the press may incur an extra charge. The amount you pay also depends on where you live, and on the sort of agency arrangement you choose. You can opt for:

- **sole agency**, whereby you instruct only one agent
- **joint agency**, whereby you instruct two agents. Both have to agree to this, and on who gets the commission on the sale
- **multiple agency**, whereby you instruct as many agents as you like: the one who comes up with the buyer earns the

commission. The fee for this type of arrangement will always be the highest.

Before you agree to an estate agent acting for you, the agent must give you specific information about its services in writing. In particular, the agent must give you advance written information about fees and charges. You must also be told about any services offered by the agent to potential buyers – such as arranging mortgages. Any technical phrases used, such as 'sole agency', must be spelt out in definitions prescribed by the Office of Fair Trading. If you are not given this information in advance, the agent will not be able to enforce payment of fees without a court order.

It is normally advisable to choose a no sale, no fee deal: that way, you pay commission only if the agent introduces you to someone who actually buys your home. Beware of contracts that say that you will have to pay the fee 'in the event of our introducing a purchaser who is able and willing to complete the transaction'. Under this arrangement, you could end up paying a fee if your home was not sold because you took it off the market, or if you found the eventual buyer yourself.

Estate agents are required to reveal promptly and in writing any personal interest they have in a transaction. During negotiations, estate agents must make sure that everyone involved is treated equally and fairly. That means, for instance, that sellers must be given written details of all offers received from potential buyers promptly – except those which the seller has told the agent not to pass on. Estate agents must also tell sellers whenever a potential buyer asks them to provide a service, such as arranging a mortgage. Lastly, it is illegal to mislead buyers or sellers in any way, by giving misleading information about offers, for instance.

Your first step with any problem should be to complain to the manager or owner of the estate agent office. If you are not happy with an estate agent, remember that you can take your house off its books. If you do not obtain satisfaction and the agent belongs to a chain, you should then write to the head office. If your problem remains unresolved, you could consider withholding part of the agent's fee. But seek advice from a Citizens Advice Bureau, Law Centre or solicitor before doing so – you might be sued by the agent, so you should be sure of your position in law.

An agent who is a member of a professional association, such as the National Association of Estate Agents, Royal Institution of Chartered Surveyors or Incorporated Society of Valuers and Auctioneers (see Addresses at the back of this book), is subject to a code of practice, and disciplinary proceedings can be taken by these bodies. So you could consider pursuing your complaint by that means – but you are unlikely to obtain compensation.

In addition, an ombudsman scheme for corporate estate agents has been set up, with a published code of practice. Under the scheme, the ombudsman can order estate agents to pay up to £1,000 compensation to a client. Unfortunately not all estate agents are part of this scheme. It is operated generally by large estate agencies. Many thousands of the smaller estate agents are not governed by the scheme, so check whether the agent that you have chosen is covered by the scheme before using that complaint procedure. If your estate agent does belong to the scheme, and your dispute remains unresolved, send details to the Estate Agents Ombudsman (see Addresses at the back of this book), requesting his involvement in the dispute. The scheme costs you nothing. If your estate agent is not a member of the scheme, your only option is to pursue your claim in court (see Chapter 17). In Scotland, solicitors often sell property and so act like estate agents. See Chapter 12 for more information about your rights against solicitors.

Problems with surveyors

Intending purchasers should always instruct a surveyor to inspect a property before exchanging contracts. The survey should reveal any defects in the property, which could prompt the purchaser to offer a lower price, or even to withdraw his offer to buy.

There are three types of survey available, differing in their depth of inspection: valuation reports, home-buyers' reports and full structural surveys. If the purchaser is getting a mortgage to fund the purchase, he will have to get at least a valuation report. These reports are for the lender's benefit, not the purchaser's. They are simply an assessment of what the property is worth and are intended to help the lender decide whether the property represents good security against the mortgage.

If the purchaser wants more information but does not want a full structural survey, he could opt for a home-buyers' report. These reports, on standard forms produced by the Royal Institution of Chartered Surveyors and the Incorporated Society of Valuers and Auctioneers, run to several pages and are divided into sections dealing with separate aspects of the structure – main walls, roofs, floors and so on. The report is intended to provide a comparatively detailed, concise account of the property.

Full structural surveys are the most thorough kind and should include a detailed description of the structure of the property, giving an account of all major and minor defects. The report should comment on all the main features of the property, from the roof to the foundations. But bear in mind that it is an inspection, not a test: while the surveyor should comment on things like wiring, plumbing, central heating and so on, he is not obliged actually to test them.

When carrying out the inspection of a property, a surveyor is under a legal duty to exercise reasonable skill and care. If the surveyor does not, and the purchaser suffers loss and damage as a direct result, then the purchaser has a claim for compensation. Strictly speaking, this is calculated as the difference in value between what was paid for the property and its true value in its defective condition.

Some surveyors' reports contain such phrases as 'we do not inspect areas that are not readily accessible' and 'we could not move furniture and therefore cannot report'. These attempts to limit the surveyor's responsibility have to be fair and reasonable. If they are not, they will be invalid under the Unfair Contract Terms Act 1977 and the Unfair Terms in Consumer Contracts Regulations 1994.

If you think that your surveyor has been negligent but he (or his insurance company) contests your claim, you may have to go to court. Negligence cases are often complicated and costly, so you should consult a solicitor – particularly if your claim falls outside the limit of the small claims procedure (see Chapter 17).

Complaining to a builder about unacceptable standards of workmanship in a new house

Dear

[Reference: address of property]

I purchased the above property from you on **[date]**. I have discovered serious defects in the quality of workmanship used in its construction **[describe]**.

I understand that under the National House Building Council Buildmark scheme, builders undertake to put right, in the first two years following purchase, any defects which result from their failure to comply with the NHBC's minimum standards of workmanship.

The defects described above indicate that this property does not conform to these standards. You are therefore in breach of your obligations under the guarantee scheme. I expect you to contact me with your proposals for remedial work within the next seven days.

Should you fail to contact me by **[date]** with proposals to put the matter right I shall refer the matter to the NHBC.

Yours sincerely

Asking the NHBC to intervene in a dispute with a builder

Dear

[Reference: builder, Buildmark guarantee number]

I am in dispute with **[builder]** regarding the unsatisfactory standard of the builder's workmanship at **[address of property]**. I enclose all the relevant documents for your information.

As you will see, I have been unable to reach a settlement with **[builder]** and so I now wish to take advantage of your conciliation scheme. I understand, however, that you will first have to write to the builder in an attempt to settle the matter without recourse to conciliation and possible arbitration.

If your intervention fails to bring about a settlement, I would be grateful if you could send me the appropriate application form for conciliation as soon as possible.

I look forward to hearing from you in due course.

Yours sincerely

encs.

Asking the NHBC to arrange for arbitration

Dear

[Reference: builder, Buildmark guarantee number]

Although I have asked **[builder]** to allow the NHBC to conciliate between us regarding the unsatisfactory building of this property, the company is not prepared to do so.

The property has serious defects **[describe]** and I would like the NHBC to arrange an arbitration hearing as soon as possible. Please send me the appropriate application form.

I look forward to hearing from you.

Yours sincerely

Withdrawing instructions to an estate agent to sell a property

Dear

[Reference: address of seller's property]

Further to our telephone conversation of **[date]**, I write to give you formal notice of the withdrawal of my instructions in connection with the sale of the above property.

Yours sincerely

Rejecting an estate agent's claim for commission

Dear

[Reference: address of seller's property]

I have received your letter of **[date]** requesting payment of the sum of **[£.....]**, representing **[..... per cent]** commission on the sale of the above property to **[purchasers]**.

We instructed **[another agent]** on **[date]**, prior to our placing instructions with you, and it was on **[date]** that **[purchasers]** first inspected our property. The fact that you subsequently issued particulars of our property to the purchasers is irrelevant, since it was **[other agent]** who introduced them to the property which they eventually bought.

I therefore reject your claim for commission.

Yours sincerely

Rejecting an estate agent's claim for commission, on a 'no sale – no commission' basis

Dear

[Reference: address of seller's property]

I have received your bill dated **[date]** for **[£.....]** commission, to which you claim that you are entitled because you introduced **[potential purchaser]** to us who was a 'buyer who was able and willing to complete the transaction'.

It was an express term of our contract that you would be paid commission only if you introduced someone to us who actually bought the property.

As you know, I asked you to take the property off the market on **[date]**. I have not sold it to **[potential purchaser]**, therefore you are not entitled to commission. Please confirm in writing that you have now taken my property off your books.

I look forward to hearing from you within the next 14 days.

Yours sincerely

Rejecting an estate agent's claim for commission on the grounds that no advance information on charges was provided

Dear

[Reference: address of seller's property]

I have received your letter of **[date]** requesting the sum of **[£.....]**, representing **[..... per cent]** agency commission on the sale of the above property to **[purchasers]**, plus costs and charges in respect of **[specify]**.

When I instructed you to handle the sale of the above property I was not given any details of the other charges you are now making in addition to your agency fees.

The Estate Agents Act 1979 and regulations and orders made under the Act require details of fees and charges, including any in addition to agency fees, to have been supplied in writing prior to my instructing you. In failing to provide such details you were breaking the law and I am not prepared to pay the sum in question unless you obtain a court order.

I am contacting my local trading standards department about this matter.

Yours sincerely

Asking the estate agents Ombudsman to intervene in a dispute

Dear

[Reference: address of seller's property]

I am writing about my dispute with **[estate agent – name and address]**, who I understand is a member of your scheme, and I enclose copies of all relevant correspondence, including the particulars that the estate agents drew up on my behalf.

I have been unable to settle the matter with **[estate agent]**, and am therefore referring the matter to you in the hope that you will be able to resolve the dispute.

I look forward to hearing from you within the next 14 days.

Yours sincerely

encs.

Complaining to a surveyor about an inadequate report on a property

Dear

[Reference: address of property surveyed]

On **[date]** your company undertook a **[type]** survey of the above on my behalf, as a result of which I proceeded with the purchase and took possession on **[date]**. On **[date]** I discovered **[problem]** requiring remedial work. The cost of this remedial work has been estimated at **[£.....]** and I hold your surveyor, **[name]**, directly responsible for this expense. These defects were present when the survey was carried out and should have been detected and commented on in the report.

Your surveyor was under a legal duty to carry out his services using a reasonable amount of skill and care, and to a reasonable level of competence. This standard has not been met, and I am legally entitled to look to you for compensation, to remedy the defects.

I expect to receive your cheque for **[£.....]** within the next 14 days. If you fail to reimburse me I shall have no alternative but to issue a summons against you in the county court for recovery of the money without further reference to you.

Yours sincerely

NOTE
Write to the surveyor before remedial work has commenced to give him a chance to inspect the damage. This is more likely to lead to a settlement of your claim than if you approach the firm once repairs have been completed.

Rejecting a surveyor's denial of liability under the terms of contractual small print

Dear

[Reference: address of property surveyed]

Thank you for your letter of **[date]**.

I am not satisfied by your claim that a clause in your survey to the effect that **[terms of clause]** relieves you of liability in this matter.

The defects that your surveyor did discover **[describe]** should have led him to investigate the property more thoroughly, and to determine the full extent of the **[defect]**. Since he did not do so, the surveyor failed to carry out his services using a reasonable amount of skill and care. Your small print is unfair and therefore invalid under the Unfair Contract Terms Act 1977 and the Unfair Terms in Consumer Contracts Regulations 1994.

I am legally entitled to redress in this matter and I expect to receive your proposals for remedying the matter at no cost to me by return.

Yours sincerely

Rejecting a surveyor's continued denial of liability

Dear

[Reference: address of property surveyed]

Thank you for your letter of **[date]**, in which you continue to deny negligence in your survey of the above property.

As you are still not prepared to accept my claim for compensation, I have no alternative but to issue a county court summons against you in the county court. I am therefore placing the matter in the hands of my solicitors, who will shortly be sending you a letter before action.

Yours sincerely

Chapter 7

Building work

MOST complaints about building work concern the price charged, the time it takes to do the job or the standard of the work.

Ask three companies to visit you to estimate the cost of the work, and discuss the job in detail with each builder when he visits your house to inspect the site. Make sure each builder is given the same information upon which to base a quote. If at all possible, use a builder recommended by a friend or relative. Also ask to see work done for other clients, and talk to them about the quality of the builder's work.

Major building work

If you are considering major building work, it can pay to instruct an architect. When you do this, the architect is placed under a legal responsibility to carry out the work with due care, skill and diligence. If the architect fails to exercise the requisite degree of skill and care, causing you to suffer loss or damage as a direct and foreseeable result, you have a claim for breach of contract.

What is required to fulfil the standard of reasonable skill and care varies according to the facts of each case. However, the starting point is always the relevant contracts. For example, the Royal Institute of British Architects (RIBA) publishes a standard form of contract called 'Appointment of an Architect'. It is also relevant to look at the surrounding circumstances. There are various codes of practice governing the professions. These broadly reflect good practice; departure from them adds to your ammunition.

The Defective Premises Act 1972 also imposes legal duties on those involved in the design or construction of homes – builders, developers, contractors, architects, surveyors and so on. It lays down that they must see that the work they take on is done in workmanlike or professional manner, with proper materials. If they don't, householders can claim under the Act. However, the cover provided by the Act is limited. A claim exists only if the defects in the home cause it to be unfit for habitation as a result of failures in design, workmanship or materials. So, many serious defects such as uneven floors, defective finishes or leaky windows might not fall within the protection given by the Act.

Also, improvement works, refurbishment and some minor types of conversion work are not covered by the Act; nor does it cover work carried out on or to an existing dwelling, falling short of the provision of the dwelling itself.

Estimates

A builder may give you a provisional price or a firm one. If the document he provides gives precise details of the work with detailed costs, the price should be binding on him. A rough price is only a general guide: when he eventually sends you his bill, the builder may charge you more. Normally, a builder's **estimate** is a rough, provisional guide to the price that will be charged when the work is complete; a **quotation** is a fixed price. If you do not agree a price in advance, you are legally obliged to pay a 'reasonable' price. What is reasonable depends on how much work has been done and the type of job that was undertaken.

Have a proper written contract drawn up between yourself and the builder, particularly for major, costly jobs. By doing so, it makes it easier to prove exactly what you and the builder agreed should any problem arise. Various organisations, such as the Joint Contracts Tribunal, produce standard contracts but they tend to be designed for large jobs.

A typical simple contract which you draw up yourself should include:

- your name and the name of the builder
- the standard of workmanship and materials to be used, including a statement that the work will be in accordance with any given

plans and specifications: these specifications may refer to appropriate British Standards or Codes of Practice

- the date on which the work will be started
- the date on which the work will be finished. You may also include a clause stating that the builder will pay you reasonable compensation if the completion is delayed. You should specify a degree of flexibility as regards the completion date, due to delays being caused by unusually bad weather or other circumstances beyond the builder's control
- a clause to the effect that the builder should leave the site in a tidy state at the end of the work
- clarification as to which party is responsible for obtaining planning permission
- precise details of how changes to specifications will be agreed
- a stipulation that the builder will be properly insured
- a precise definition of circumstances in which you or the builder can terminate the contract
- the total cost of the work and how the bill will be paid – in a lump sum at the end, or in stage payments as the work progresses
- a requirement that the builder return to put right any defects that manifest themselves in the work after it is completed, and to rectify any damage caused to your property, at his expense.

If the builder offers his own contract for the work, you should read its small print very carefully and check it against this list before signing. If the builder has reservations about the contract you want to use, discuss it to see if you can reach a sensible compromise.

Coping with delays

If it is important to you that the work is completed by a particular date, get the builder to agree in writing to a specific date for completion of the work, and also make clear in writing that 'time is of the essence'. By doing so you give yourself stronger legal rights in the event of the work not being finished on time – if the builder does not complete the job on time, you could, for example, cancel the contract and call in another builder to complete the work; if this costs you more than the first builder's estimate, you can claim the extra cost from the original firm.

The law does not normally regard time as a crucial element of building contracts, so if the work is not done on time, and you have not agreed that time is of the essence, you may claim compensation for breach of contract – if you have suffered financially as a result of the delay e.g. you have been compelled to eat out because of the unfinished state of your kitchen – but the contract will still stand and you will not be entitled to call in another builder to finish the job.

If you have not agreed a completion date, you are entitled to have the work carried out within a reasonable time. This period is not defined by law but it depends on the size and type of work involved. So if the work is delayed you should give the builder written notice that you are making time of the essence and fix a reasonable date for completion. Then if the work is not finished on time you can safely consider the contract at an end.

Faulty workmanship

Every time a builder agrees to carry out work for a client, the client enters into a contract with him. Along with the specific rights given in the contract (for example, the types of materials that the builder should use) the client also has rights under the Supply of Goods and Services Act 1982 (common law in Scotland), which entitle the client to have the work carried out with reasonable skill and care, and within a reasonable time. If the builder does not carry out work as specifically agreed in the contract (if he uses the wrong type of roof tiles, for example) or does not carry out the work with reasonable skill and care, the client can claim for breach of contract. This means that he is legally entitled to have the work put right free of charge.

Calling in another contractor

If the builder does not put the work right, the client should get two or three quotations for remedying the problem and send these to the first builder. This shows he is serious and will, if necessary, call in another builder to carry out remedial work.

Getting the cost back

If the client eventually has to get another firm to put the work right, he is legally entitled to claim the cost of their work from the original firm. But he may need evidence from an expert to substantiate his claim. He can get this from the firm that does the repairs, by asking the repairer for a written diagnosis of what was wrong.

Asking a builder to submit an estimate for a job

Dear

[Reference: brief description of job]

Further to our telephone conversation of **[date]**, I would like you to give me an estimate for **[precise details of service required]** at **[address]**.

Please confirm a date and time for your visit to undertake a detailed estimate.

I look forward to hearing from you within the next seven days.

Yours sincerely

Rejecting a builder's bill for more than the original quotation

Dear

[Reference: estimate number]

I was surprised to see from your invoice **[number]** of **[date]** that the cost of **[work and fittings: describe]** is **[£.....]**, **[£.....]** higher than that in your firm's original quotation of **[£.....]** of **[date]**, which set out the fixed price for the work and which was the basis upon which I entered into a contract with you.

Though you claim the increase is due to **[factors, describe]**, this has no bearing on our contract. There was no agreement between us at the time I commissioned your firm to carry out the work that I should bear the cost of **[external factors: describe if appropriate]**. We agreed an exact price for the work and therefore my contractual obligation is simply to the contracted price shown in your quotation.

I therefore enclose a cheque for **[£.....]**, being the amount of the original estimate, in full and final settlement.

Yours sincerely

encs.

Complaining to a builder about delays in completing a job

Dear

[Reference: estimate number]

I am extremely concerned about your delay in completing the **[work]** contracted for the above property **[address if different from letterhead]**.

Prior to my accepting your estimate for the job, I was assured that the work would be completed by **[date]**. **[.....]** weeks/months later, the work is incomplete **[details of work still to be done]**.

I am therefore making time of the essence in this contract. If your firm does not complete the outstanding work within 14 days of the date of this letter, I shall consider the contract between us to be at an end, as I am legally entitled to do. I shall then instruct another firm to complete the work, deducting the cost from the balance requested in your invoice.

Yours sincerely

Responding to a builder's continued failure to complete work on time

Dear

[Reference: estimate number]

Further to my letter of **[date]**, in which I made time of the essence, I am disappointed that you have not replied to my letter and have failed to complete the work in the time stipulated.

In the circumstances I am left with no alternative but to consider our contract at an end.

In accordance with my legal rights, I now intend to have the work completed by another contractor at your expense. I am therefore obtaining estimates from other contractors and shall forward copies to you in due course.

Yours sincerely

Deducting the cost of subsequent builder's work from the initial builder's bill

Dear

[Reference: estimate number]

On **[date]** I sent you **[.....]** estimates from builders who were prepared to complete the work left unfinished by your company. Since you have not responded to any of my letters, I was compelled to engage **[contractor]**, who provided the lowest estimate. The bill for completing the job was **[£.....]**.

Since I incurred this expenditure as a direct result of your breach of contract, I am legally entitled to look to you to meet the cost of the work. I am therefore deducting **[£.....]** from the balance of **[£.....]** due to your firm.

I enclose a cheque for **[£.....]** in full and final settlement for the work your company carried out on my property.

Yours sincerely

encs.

Asking a builder to rectify his defective workmanship

Dear

[Reference: estimate number]

On **[date]** you undertook **[work]** at the above address. On **[date]** this work proved defective: **[describe]**.

It was implied in the contract between us that you would carry out the work with reasonable skill and care and would use materials of a reasonable quality. This is laid down by the Supply of Goods and Services Act 1982. The above defect shows that you have failed to fulfil these legal obligations. I therefore have a claim against you for breach of contract.

However, while reserving my rights to claim against you, I am prepared to give you an opportunity to carry out free repairs to rectify the matter within a reasonable time at no charge to me.

If you do not carry out the necessary remedial work within 14 days, I shall have no alternative but to retain another contractor to put the matter right and look to you to bear the cost of the work, as I am legally entitled to do.

Yours sincerely

NOTE
When you give the builder a chance to put the work right, make sure you keep your rights open by saying at the outset that you are 'reserving your rights'. That way you can still claim if the job is done badly.

Informing a builder that you are appointing another builder to rectify his defective workmanship

Dear

[Reference: estimate number]

Since you have failed to carry out the repairs to my property within the time specified in my letter of **[date]** I have had no alternative but to obtain estimates from other contractors, namely **[contractors]**; copies of these estimates are enclosed.

As you will see, the estimates show that the work you did **[describe]** is defective and needs extensive repair. These repairs will cost at least **[£.....]**, as indicated on the lowest of the **[.....]** estimates. I am legally entitled to expect you to pay for this work, and I therefore look forward to receiving your proposals for settlement by return.

Yours sincerely

encs.

Claiming the cost of subsequent repairs from a builder whose workmanship was defective

Dear

[Reference: estimate number]

Since you failed to reply to my letter of **[date]** I had no alternative but to engage **[contractor]** to carry out the remedial work necessitated by the substandard nature of your original work. That work is now complete and has cost **[£.....]**. A copy of the firm's invoice is enclosed for your information.

You will also see that I have enclosed a copy of a report I asked **[contractor]** to prepare on the work required, which shows that the work carried out by you was substandard. As it was not carried out with due skill, I have a claim against you for breach of contract. In the circumstances I am exercising my legal right to expect you to reimburse me with the cost of repairs, **[£.....]**.

I look forward to receiving your cheque within the next 14 days. If you fail to reimburse me I shall have no alternative but to issue a summons against you in the county court for recovery of the money without further reference to you.

Yours sincerely

encs.

NOTE
If this does not settle the claim, send a letter before action, threatening court action (see Chapter 17).

Sending a builder a letter before action

Dear

[Reference: estimate number]

Further to my letter of **[date]**, to which you have not replied, I write to inform you that, unless I receive your satisfactory proposals for settlement of my outstanding claim within seven days of the date of this letter, I intend to issue a summons against you in the county court, without further reference to you.

Yours sincerely

NOTE
If this letter does not resolve the matter and the sum involved is under £5,000 (£1,000 in N. Ireland, £750 in Scotland) (see Chapter 17), issue a summons in the small claims court; otherwise consult a solicitor.

Complaining about work carried out by an architect

.Dear

[Reference: address where work is taking place]

I am writing to complain about the service you provided when I instructed you to prepare the following plans **[describe]** for, and supervise the work at, the above address.

When I first spoke to you on **[date]**, I made it clear that I wanted the work to proceed as follows **[describe]**. It has now become apparent that the service you have provided is deficient in the following respects **[describe]**.

The Royal Institute of British Architects standard form of contract covering our agreement, 'Appointment of an Architect', provides as follows **[set out specific clauses that the architect has not followed]**. Also, the Supply of Goods and Services Act 1982 requires you to carry out your service as an architect with reasonable skill and care. The problems described above show that you failed in your legal obligations. I therefore have a claim against you for breach of contract.

Because of your breach of contract I have suffered the following loss **[describe]**.

I consider that **[£.....]** would be a reasonable sum of compensation for your failure to meet your legal obligations. I therefore look forward to receiving your cheque within the next 14 days.

Yours sincerely

Complaining to an architect under the Defective Premises Act

Dear

[Reference: address where work is taking place]

I am writing to complain about the service you provided when I instructed you to prepare the following plans **[describe]** for, and supervise the work at, the above address.

When I first spoke to you on **[date]**, I made it clear that I wanted the work to proceed as follows **[describe]**.

The Defective Premises Act 1972 also imposes a legal duty on you to see that the work was done in a workmanlike or professional manner, with proper materials. Also, the Supply of Goods and Services Act 1982 requires you to carry out your service as an architect with reasonable skill and care.

The problems and defects described above have caused my home to be unfit for habitation. This clearly shows that you have failed in your legal obligations. I therefore have a claim against you for breach of contract.

Because of your breach of contract I have suffered the following loss **[describe]**.

I consider that **[£.....]** would be a reasonable sum of compensation for your failure to meet your legal obligations. I therefore look forward to receiving your cheque within the next 14 days.

Yours sincerely

Chapter 8

Commercial services

Dry-cleaners

The Supply of Goods and Services Act 1982 (common law in Scotland) entitles you to have dry-cleaning carried out with reasonable skill and care. If the dry-cleaner provides a service which does not meet these standards, you can claim compensation. Generally, you are entitled to claim the cost of replacing the damaged or missing item, though you may find that the amount of compensation is reduced to take into account wear and tear of the garment.

If a problem arises, write to the dry-cleaner in the first instance. If this does not sort out the problem, but the firm belongs to the Textile Services Association (TSAL), write to that body (see Addresses at the back of this book). If your clothes have been damaged or unsatisfactorily processed due to the dry-cleaner's negligence, either they will be cleaned free of charge, or the association will conciliate between you and the dry-cleaners in your claim for compensation. You may be asked to prove your claim, in which case you can make use of the association's testing service on a 'loser pays' basis, if both you and the dry-cleaner agree to it. The association also operates an arbitration service for unresolved disputes.

If the firm is not a member of the TSAL and fails to offer compensation, pursue the matter as a small claim in the county court.

Photoprocessors

The Supply of Goods and Services Act 1982 (common law in

Scotland) gives you rights when you have films processed. If your photographs of a once-in-a-lifetime holiday, for example, are lost or damaged by a photoprocessor, you are entitled to claim compensation for the value of the film and for the loss of enjoyment which you would have had from the photographs had they been processed correctly. The amount of compensation to claim depends upon the importance to you of the photographs that have been lost or damaged. You will get more compensation for lost films of your own wedding, for example, than for those of a distant relative's birthday celebrations. The loss of photographs of your silver wedding or of your child receiving the gold award in the Duke of Edinburgh's award scheme could result in your receiving compensation of around £200 at current values. If the photographs are not of a unique event and their subject can easily be photographed again, you are entitled to claim only the cost of a replacement film and the cost of postage.

Photoprocessors often claim that they are not liable to pay compensation, alleging that their obligations are limited by the terms of the small print on the film's packaging. Do not be deterred by this argument. To be legally binding small print has to be fair and reasonable, as laid down by the Unfair Contract Terms Act 1977 and the Unfair Terms in Consumer Contracts Regulations 1994. Most photoprocessors now use small print which says that films that are very valuable to you may be processed separately for an extra charge, or which advises you to take out your own insurance. The reasonableness, in the legal sense, of these clauses depends on the size and legibility of the small print and the alternative sorts of services offered by the firm to consumers.

Removal companies

When you instruct a removal company to move your household possessions, you are entitled to have the service performed with reasonable skill and care. This is laid down by the Supply of Goods and Services Act 1982 (common law in Scotland). If the company does not carry out the service properly – if crockery packed by its staff gets broken, for example – you are legally entitled to claim against the firm for breach of contract.

Broken appointments

If you instruct a removal company to collect your possessions at a precise time and date, and it fails to turn up on time or at all, despite having agreed to do so, you have a claim against it for breach of contract. You are entitled to cancel the contract and to hire another removal company to move your possessions.

Removal firms have a trade association, the British Association of Removers (see Addresses at the back of this book), which aims to resolve complaints against its members by conciliating between the parties involved, if they agree to it. It will also appoint an independent arbitrator if both parties agree to it.

Hairdressers and beauticians

Hairdressers and beauticians provide a service. Again, the Supply of Goods and Services Act 1982 (common law in Scotland) entitles you to have the service performed with reasonable skill and care and with materials of a reasonable quality. So, when carrying out a chemical treatment to your hair, for example, a competent hairdresser should first carry out a patch test on a small section of your scalp to test for any adverse reaction. If the hairdresser does not do this and you suffer injury as a result, you have a claim for compensation for pain and suffering and any other loss you have suffered as a result.

If your complaint is about a serious problem, take photos of what has gone wrong and the injuries you have suffered. Also, get a GP's opinion backing your case. If the problem is particularly serious, you may be referred to a specialist, such as a dermatologist or trichologist.

If the hairdresser with whom you are unable to sort out a complaint is a member of the Hairdressing Council (look in the salon for a logo), you may be able to use this trade association's conciliation and arbitration scheme. The Council also has the power to deregister a hairdresser and the threat of this may help speed up the settlement of your dispute.

Complaining to a dry-cleaners about damage caused by its service

Dear

I am writing about the damage to **[item: type, make, fabric, colour etc.]** caused by your establishment on **[date]**.

The Supply of Goods and Services Act 1982 requires you to carry out your service as a dry-cleaner in a good and workmanlike manner, using that degree of skill and care reasonably to be expected from a firm purporting to be experienced in the work. The damage to the above item **[describe]** is evidence that you have failed to exercise your duty when undertaking cleaning on my behalf.

You are required by law to compensate me for my loss and I therefore look forward to receiving your proposals for settlement within 14 days.

Yours sincerely

Asking the dry-cleaners' trade association to intervene in a dispute

Dear

[Reference: dry-cleaning establishment]

I am in dispute with the above company over the damage caused to **[item]** when in its possession. I enclose copies of all the relevant correspondence.

As I have been unable to reach a settlement with **[establishment]** I now wish to take advantage of your advisory and conciliation service.

I therefore look forward to hearing from you in due course.

Yours sincerely

encs.

Claiming compensation from a photoprocessor for damaged photographs

Dear

On **[date]** I sent you **[description of film]** for processing, but it was damaged **[describe how]** while in your possession.

The ruined photographs represented **[describe]** and by the nature of the event are irreplaceable.

Under the Supply of Goods and Services Act 1982 you were obliged to ensure that the film was processed with reasonable skill and care. The above damage shows that you failed to meet your legal obligations.

I am legally entitled to receive compensation from you for the value of the film and for the loss of enjoyment which would have been derived from the record of this once-in-a-lifetime event.

I consider that **[£.....]** would be a reasonable sum of compensation for your failure to meet your legal obligations. I therefore look forward to receiving your cheque within the next 14 days.

Yours sincerely

Rejecting a photoprocessor's unacceptable offer of compensation

Dear

Thank you for your letter of **[date]** offering me **[terms of compensation]**.

I am not prepared to accept your offer, and I reject your claim that your obligations are limited by the small print on the packaging of your films. As the small print on the mailing envelope was almost illegible and did not make it clear that different types of service were available, it was unfair and unreasonable and ineffective, as defined by the Unfair Contract Terms Act 1977 and the Unfair Terms in Consumer Contracts Regulations 1994.

I am therefore entitled to receive proper compensation for the damaged films, and I expect you to pay me the **[£.....]** that I claimed in my letter of **[date]**, within the next 14 days.

Yours sincerely

NOTE
If the photoprocessor still fails to settle your claim, your only option is to pursue the matter in the county court (see Chapter 17).

Complaining to a removal company about damage to possessions caused in transit

Dear

[Reference: removal order number]

I am writing to you about the damage to **[property: describe]** caused when you moved my possessions from **[location]** to **[location]** on **[date]** which I pointed out to your staff when my possessions were unloaded.

The Supply of Goods and Services Act 1982 requires you to carry out your services with reasonable skill and care. The above damage indicates that you failed to fulfil these legal obligations when undertaking the work. I therefore have a claim against you for breach of contract.

However, while reserving my rights, I am prepared to give you an opportunity to arrange for the necessary remedial work to restore the **[items]** to their former good condition within a reasonable time.

Please let me know within the next 14 days what arrangements you intend to make to remedy your breach of contract.

Yours sincerely

Complaining to a removal company about its failure to keep an appointment

Dear

[Reference: removal order number]

On **[date]** I made a booking with your firm to collect items from **[location]** at **[time]** on **[date]** and deliver to **[location]** on **[date]**.

Your failure to collect at the agreed time constitutes a breach of contract. I am therefore entitled to claim compensation from you not only for my out-of-pocket expenses **[describe]**, but also for the substantial inconvenience I suffered in having to make alternative arrangements for this delivery to take place **[describe]**.

In the circumstances, I expect to receive compensation of **[£.....]** within 14 days.

Yours sincerely

Complaining to a hairdresser about damage to your hair

Dear

I am writing to you about the damage to my scalp and hair caused by you when you [describe treatment]. Shortly after a I received the treatment, it became apparent that I was suffering from the following problems [describe].

The Supply of Goods and Services Act 1982 requires you to carry out your service as a hairdresser with reasonable skill and care, using materials of a reasonable quality. The problems described above show that you failed in your legal obligations. I therefore have a claim against you for breach of contract.

Because of your breach of contract I have suffered the following injuries [describe, together with any consequences, such as medical treatment, absence from work and so on].

I consider that [£.....] would be a reasonable sum of compensation for your failure to meet your legal obligations. I therefore look forward to receiving your cheque within the next 14 days.

Yours sincerely

Asking the Hairdressing Council to intervene in a dispute with a hairdresser

Dear

[Reference: name of salon]

I am in dispute with the above named salon concerning the service I received from it on **[date]**.

I enclose copies of the relevant correspondence. As you will see, the treatment I received from the salon caused the following injuries **[describe, together with any consequences, such as medical treatment, absence from work and so on]**.

I contacted the salon on **[date]** to complain about this matter but the dispute has not been resolved to my satisfaction.

Since the salon is a member of the Council I am now referring the matter to you for investigation. I look forward to hearing from you in due course.

Yours sincerely

encs.

Chapter 9

Domestic services

Electricity

Since the passing of the Electricity Act 1989, domestic consumers have been receiving their electricity from public electricity suppliers instead of from the old area electricity boards. If you have a complaint about a bill or your electricity supply, first get in touch with your electricity supplier. If your first approach does not resolve your problem, write to your local Office of Electricity Regulation (OFFER) at the address on your bill.

OFFER is an independent regulatory body set up to monitor electricity suppliers and to ensure that they comply with their statutory obligations. Following the privatisation of the industry by the Electricity Act 1989, OFFER has instituted guaranteed standards of performance.

The scheme includes compensation of a fixed sum, currently £20, for householders who suffer power cuts of 24 hours (plus £10 for every further 12 hours without power), if these result from technical breakdowns or negligence, but not when severe weather is the cause. If an engineer fails to keep an appointment, customers receive another sum, currently £10. Various delays (in giving customers notice of supply interruptions, dealing with company fuse failures, giving estimates of connection charges, and in dealing with meter problems, voltage complaints and charges and payment queries) also attract compensation. Payments are automatic for most of the standards and are normally made by reducing the customer's next electricity bill (though for delayed supply restoration and lack of notice of supply interruption, it is necessary to submit a claim).

Some electricity suppliers already offer rebate and voucher schemes so check by writing to the address on your bill.

For Northern Ireland, contact your local Northern Ireland Electricity Office (see phone book). If you are not satisfied, contact the General Consumer Council for Northern Ireland (see Addresses at the back of the book).

Checking the accuracy of the meter

Before being installed, all electricity meters are examined and checked for accuracy by a qualified meter examiner and are then certified as working correctly. The electricity supplier therefore assumes that the meter still records usage accurately, and that its readings, and the bills derived from them, are correct.

There are two ways of challenging the electricity supplier's assumption. One is to show that what you regard as abnormally high readings are caused by a 'leakage to earth'. This can be established by turning off all your electrical appliances, then checking to see if the meter is still recording electricity usage. Another solution is to ask the supplier to check the accuracy of the meter. Charges for this range from under £20 to £50 depending on the company and the type of test carried out, and will be refunded if the metre is faulty.

After the electricity supplier's meter test, you can refer the matter to OFFER, either directly or through your electricity supplier. If you apply direct to OFFER, you should inform your supplier that you have made the application. OFFER will then nominate an independent Meter Examiner to visit your home to test your meter and installation, and if necessary to take away the disputed meter for further tests (replacing it with a new certified meter). He will subsequently send his conclusion and report to OFFER, which will in turn contact you.

If you are dissatisfied with OFFER's decision, you will have to pursue the matter in court. However, your chances of success will be slight: it will be extremely difficult to prove that the Meter Examiner's report is incorrect.

Gas

More and more gas consumers have a choice of gas supplier, with different companies competing to supply gas to homes and to service gas equipment. Check your bills or supply contract to see who to complain to if you have problems. Still, if you buy goods from a gas showroom, you have the same rights as you would have in dealing with any other retailer, as laid down by the Sale of Goods Act 1979.

Similarly, if you have had your central heating installed or serviced by a gas supplier or a fitter registered with CORGI (the Council for Registered Gas Fitters), you have the same rights as you would have with any other contractor, under the Supply of Goods and Services Act 1982 (common law in Scotland): you are entitled to have the service performed with reasonable skill and care.

If you want to complain about a gas bill, an appliance or a service, write initially to your local gas office. If you are not satisfied with the reply you receive, contact the Customer Relations Manager at the regional services area service centre (for British Gas, see Addresses at the back of the book), or the Gas Consumers Council (GCC) for your region (the address is on the back of your bill), or write to its head office (see Addresses at the back of this book). The GCC was established by the Gas Act 1986 to represent the interests of all gas consumers. It has wide responsibilities for investigating gas problems, including the servicing and installation of gas appliances.

If the GCC cannot get a settlement to your satisfaction then it will pass the details to OFGAS, the Office of Gas Supply (see Addresses at the back of this book), an independent regulatory body which monitors the activities of gas suppliers and has the power to ensure that they comply with their statutory obligations. OFGAS may, for example, intervene in cases of proposed or actual disconnection where a supplier has contravened its duty to give and continue a supply to a customer's home. Remember that suppliers are entitled to disconnect a supply for non-payment of a gas bill, though cases of hardship should be dealt with reasonably and sensitively.

Fixed compensation scheme

Early in 1992, British Gas launched a new campaign on standards of service, 'Commitment to Customers'. In many cases, if British Gas fails to meet its targets you can get fixed compensation. The compensation scheme includes:

- **missed appointments** – you receive £10 compensation if British Gas fails to turn up for an appointment, unless it gave you 24 hours' notice that it could not keep the appointment.
- **interruptions of gas supply for safety reasons** – British Gas promises £20 compensation for each day or part of the day you are without gas, if the supply is not restored within one working day; and
- **special treatment for older and disabled customers** – £10 compensation if British Gas cuts off the gas supply to an older, disabled or otherwise vulnerable customer, and leaves him or her without adequate heating and cooking facilities.

Full details of the scheme can be obtained free from your local gas showroom, or district regional office.

Water

In England and Wales, the activities of every water company are regulated by a code of practice. This sets out what services are offered, gives details of charges, tells customers what to do in an emergency and lays down a procedure for making complaints. There are also codes of practice covering leakage and disconnection. Leaflets explaining all these codes are available from your local water company: look under Water in the telephone directory or ask OFWAT – the Office of Water Services (see Addresses at the back of this book), the statutory watch-dog set up to ensure that both consumers of water and the environment are properly protected.

Following the Water Act 1989 water companies are legally obliged to operate a Guaranteed Standards Scheme. Customers are entitled to claim a set amount, currently £5, every time there are unplanned interruptions of water supply lasting longer than a specified time, or if it takes longer to restore the water supply than the customer was told. You may also claim this amount if your water company does not keep appointments on the date agreed in writing, or if there is no answer to your complaint or enquiry within a specified period.

If you cannot get satisfaction from the water company, write to the Office of Water Services' Customer Service Committee for your area (the address is in the telephone directory under Office of Water Services). If its intervention does not resolve the problem to your satisfaction, you can ask for your complaint to be passed to OFWAT's Director General.

In Scotland, write to the water authority for your area. If you are still not happy, write to the Scottish Water and Sewerage Customers' Council (see Addresses at the back of this book).

In Northern Ireland, contact the Water Services Office of the Department of the Environment.

Unwholesome water

Water companies are under a legal obligation to maintain a supply of wholesome water, as laid down by the Water Act 1989. If yours does not, write to its head office, claiming compensation for any inconvenience you may have suffered.

Telephones

If you decide to dispute your telephone bill, the first step is to complain to your local BT office – its address is on your telephone bill – or to your phone operator if you have switched to a competitor. Once you have submitted your written complaint, the phone operator will usually test the meter and check the readings (which are recorded on film) to trace any inaccuracy in the metering. It will also check for any recently located faults in the network that could have affected the metering at the exchange responsible for your line.

If you have already tried this course of action and are not satisfied with its outcome, consult your National Advisory Committee (at the address in the back of your local telephone book). While the complaint is being considered, the phone operator will not sue you for non-payment. If necessary, the dispute can then be taken up by the Office of Telecommunications, the statutory body empowered by law to ensure that all telephone operators meet their obligations under their respective licences, and to provide advice and assistance to telephone users (see Addresses at the back of this book).

If you have exhausted all the complaints procedures but still wish to pursue your claim, you can either use arbitration if the operator offers it (BT does) or take the case to court.

The Chartered Institute of Arbitrators, which is totally independent of BT, for example, provides legally binding arbitration. All the evidence is submitted in writing so you do not have to attend a hearing to present your evidence in person as you would before a court of law. The decision of the arbitrator is legally binding on both you and BT, say, so you will not be allowed to start legal proceedings if you do not agree with the outcome of arbitration. You will have to pay a fee with your application, at present £15, which will probably be refunded if the arbitrator finds in your favour (this is left to his discretion). You do not have to pay any other costs.

Telephone customer service guarantee scheme

Under its guarantee scheme British Telecom promises an agreed date of appointment for installation of your telephone line. It also guarantees to repair line faults by the end of the day following the one when they were reported. If BT falls short of its installation and repair targets, including weekends, you can claim compensation of one month's line rental charge per day. Alternatively, if you suffer financial loss as a result of BT's failure to meet its targets, you can claim up to £1,000 compensation.

You have four months in which to register a claim.

Complaining to an electricity company about meter readings

Dear

[Reference: account number and bill]

Thank you for your letter of **[date]** concerning the above account.

I do not accept that the meter is recording accurately. The bill in question **[reference]** for **[£.....]** reflects a greater than usual usage, but owing to **[circumstances: absence etc.]**, it should be less than usual.

I inspected the meter with all my electrical appliances turned off and noted that it continued to register **[.....]** units of electricity consumption. It is clear that either the meter is faulty or that there is a leakage to earth, so the bill is not a true reflection of electricity used. I now wish to request you to carry out a test on the electricity meter at my home.

I look forward to hearing from you with a suitable date for the test to be carried out.

Yours sincerely

Asking OFFER to intervene in a dispute with an electricity company

Dear

[Reference: account number and bill]

I am writing with reference to my dispute with the **[utility company]** which has yet to be settled to my satisfaction.

I am enclosing copies of all the recent bills and correspondence relating to the above account. As you will see, it appears that the meter is not recording correctly, because **[summarise argument]**.

I therefore wish you to intervene on my behalf. I understand that while you are considering the matter no legal action will be taken over non-payment of the bill, nor will my electricity supply be disconnected.

I look forward to hearing from you in due course.

Yours sincerely

encs.

Complaining to a gas company about a high bill

Dear

[Reference: account number]

I wish to complain about your bill dated **[date]** for **[amount]** which I received today.

This bill is unusually high, and I have reason to doubt its accuracy because **[details]**. I believe the gas meter in my home is defective.

Please check the bill again and arrange for an inspection of the meter at my home.

I look forward to hearing from you with a suitable date for the test to be carried out.

Yours sincerely

Asking the Gas Consumers Council to intervene in a dispute

Dear

[Reference: gas company and account number]

I am in dispute with the above supplier concerning my bill **[date; reference if any]** for **[£.....]**.

I am enclosing copies of the relevant bills and correspondence relating to the above account. As you will see, I believe that the gas meter at my home is not working properly because **[details]** and I would like you to intervene on my behalf.

I look forward to hearing from you in due course.

Yours sincerely

encs.

Complaining to a gas company about defective servicing

Dear

[Reference: account number]

On **[date]** your engineer called to carry out a service of my gas central heating system **[details of system]**. Since then the system has exhibited defects: **[describe]**.

The Supply of Goods and Services Act 1982 requires you to carry out this servicing in a good and workmanlike manner, using that degree of skill and care reasonably to be expected from a firm purporting to be experienced in the work. The above defects show that you have failed to fulfil your legal obligations.

However, while reserving my rights, I am prepared to give you one last opportunity to undertake the necessary remedial work to bring the job up to a reasonable standard within a reasonable time.

If you do not carry out the remedial work within 14 days, I shall have no alternative but to retain another contractor to put the matter right and to look to you to bear the cost of the work, as I am legally entitled to do.

Yours sincerely

NOTE
If this does not resolve your problem, obtain three quotations from qualified Council for Registered Gas Installers (CORGI) gas fitters, and send them to the supplier. If this does not resolve the matter, get the work put right by the gas fitter tendering the lowest quotation and send his bill to the supplier. If the supplier refuses to reimburse you for this, you can issue a small claims summons.

Complaining to a water company about a break in water supply

Dear

[Reference: account number]

I am writing to confirm our telephone conversation of **[date]** to the effect that the supply of water to my home was interrupted for a period of **[.....]** days from **[date]** to **[date]** inclusive.

Under the Water Act 1989, you are obliged to provide a supply of water that is sufficient for my domestic purposes. As you failed in this duty I am entitled to compensation for the loss and damage I suffered as a result, which were as follows: **[describe]**. I am enclosing copies of receipts for the necessary remedial work and reports from the repairers confirming that the damage arose from the insufficient supply of water.

I am also legally entitled under the above Act to claim compensation of £5 for each day that I was without water.

I look forward to receiving your proposals for compensation within 14 days of the date of this letter.

Yours sincerely

encs.

Asking OFWAT to intervene in a dispute with a water company

Dear

[Reference: water company and account number]

I am in dispute with the above company concerning the water supply to my home.

I enclose copies of the relevant correspondence. As you will see, on **[date]** the water supply to my home became unwholesome **[describe]**. This problem lasted for **[.....]** days. I contacted the **[supplier]** on **[date]** to complain about this matter but the dispute has not been resolved to my satisfaction.

I understand that the water company is obliged under the Water Act 1989 to maintain a supply of wholesome water I therefore ask you to obtain for me the appropriate compensation for the inconvenience I have suffered.

I look forward to hearing from you in due course.

Yours sincerely

encs.

Complaining to a phone operator about a high telephone bill

Dear

[Reference: account number]

I am writing to you in connection with your bill relating to the above account, for **[£.....]** covering **[period]**, which is unacceptably high and which does not reflect the use I have made of the telephone.

My reasons for disputing it are as follows: **[describe]**. As I believe the meter on my line must be faulty, I would like you to arrange to have it tested for accuracy as soon as possible.

I look forward to hearing from you with proposed dates for this testing.

Yours sincerely

Asking the Office of Telecommunications (OFTEL) to intervene in a dispute

Dear

[Reference: number: bill date]

I am in dispute with **[phone operator]** about the above telephone bill, which is unacceptably high. My reasons for disputing the amount are as follows: **[describe]** and I am not satisfied with the phone operator's response to the effect that **[summarise]**.

I enclose copies of all relevant correspondence and bills and would ask you to intervene on my behalf.

I look forward to your response in due course.

Yours sincerely

encs.

Claiming compensation for inconvenience from British Telecom

Dear

[Reference: account number]

On **[date]** I reported to you that there was a fault on my telephone line **[telephone number]** whereby **[describe]**. I was told that the matter would be resolved by **[date]**. This did not prove to be the case and **[describe subsequent events]** meant that the fault was not remedied until **[date]**.

Under your Customer Service Guarantee, I am entitled to claim for compensation for inconvenience caused by interruptions of service, and I look forward to receiving your proposals for compensation within the next 14 days. If I do not hear from you within that period I will refer the matter to the Office of Telecommunications.

Yours sincerely

NOTE
If the problem is not resolved, contact your National Advisory Committee or OFTEL.

Chapter 10

Finance

RECENT Acts of Parliament, culminating in the Financial Services Act 1986, have made enormous changes in the consumer's legal position when borrowing money, buying on credit and making use of other financial services. This section also focuses on banks, accountants and the protection given to consumers by the Consumer Credit Act 1974, which protects individual borrowers in a number of ways. In order to fall within the Act's jurisdiction, an agreement for credit must not exceed £15,000. Agreements to borrow money to buy land, and certain charge card agreements such as those operated by American Express and Diners Club, are not covered.

Being turned down for credit

No organisation is obliged to lend you money or give you credit, nor does it have to tell you why it will not do so. But there is nothing to stop you asking for your application to be reconsidered.

You have rights laid down by Sections 157–60 of the Consumer Credit Act 1974 which allow you to challenge the basis of a credit company's rejection of your application. If you write within 28 days of the notification of a credit refusal to the company which refused you credit, asking whether a credit reference agency has been used in considering your application, the company is obliged to tell you whether such an agency has been used and to give you its name and address. You can then write to the agency, requesting a copy of the file relating to your case. The agency is obliged to send you a copy of it for a fee, currently £1. If the information on the file is incorrect, you are entitled to have it amended or removed, and to receive notice within 28 days of pointing out the error that this has been done. Once the information has been corrected, you can re-apply for credit.

Rebate on early settlement

Most consumer loan agreements are credit agreements regulated by the Consumer Credit Act 1974. Check the small print on your agreement; if the agreement is regulated by the Act, the small print will say so. This gives you two related rights:

(1) to pay off all amounts due at any time during the duration of the agreement, and
(2) to receive a rebate of the credit charges taking into account the earlier receipt of the money by the creditor.

In order to exercise the right of early settlement, you must send **written** notice to the creditor and pay off all you owe under the agreement, less any rebate allowable. Details of the various calculations governing the rebates allowed in the various types of loan agreement are set out in the Consumer Credit Regulations. The mathematics involved is complicated and is worked out by the credit company.

In order to help you exercise your right of early settlement, regulations under the Act say that the creditor is under a duty, once he has received written notice from the borrower, to supply you with a statement showing how much needs to be paid, and showing the basic calculations involved in arriving at that sum. This statement will not necessarily show all the details of that calculation. If a complete breakdown is required, request this in writing from the Office of Fair Trading (see Addresses at the back of this book).

If the creditor is considering your complaint, you can apply to the county court (Sheriff Court in Scotland) for the credit agreement to be re-opened and the terms of the agreement to be re-written. Take legal advice from a solicitor before applying to the court to have the agreement re-opened and re-written.

Extortionate credit

If your loan payments are exorbitant, or if the rate of interest you are being charged is very high, you are legally entitled to ask the creditor to reconsider the matter. Your right to do so is laid out in Sections 137–40 of the Consumer Credit Act 1974.

Credit card rights

Paying by credit card, such as Access or Visa, gives you the added protection of the Consumer Credit Act 1974, provided the goods cost over £100. If you pay by this means, the credit card company as well as the retailer is liable for any breach of contract. So you can claim for faulty goods against the retailer, the credit card company or both. We advise you to write to both parties when you are making your claim. You will not get two lots of compensation, but you will increase your chances of getting the problem sorted out.

You are also entitled to claim from the credit card company if the retailer goes into liquidation. This cover is particularly useful if you have made a payment in advance, such as a deposit, to a company that subsequently closes down, for you would otherwise have to take your chances as an unsecured creditor.

Buying on hire purchase

If you buy something on hire purchase, your contract is with the finance company, the lender, *not* the retailer who supplied the goods.

In such transactions, you have the same basic rights as if you had paid cash: it is implied in the credit agreement that the goods will correspond to any description given of them by the salesman or in sales literature; will be of satisfactory quality and, if you relied upon the retailer's judgement because you required the goods for a particular purpose, they should be reasonably fit for that purpose for which you acquired them. With hire purchase, these rights are laid down by the Supply of Goods (Implied Terms) Act 1973.

When it comes to rejecting faulty goods your rights last longer if you have bought on HP than if you have bought them for cash. If you are paying on HP, you have the common law right to reject faulty goods *throughout* the duration of the agreement. If you find a problem with the goods and want to reject them, stop paying the instalments, write to the HP company and state what the problem is – that the goods are unsatisfactory, for example, that you are rejecting them, and that they are available for collection by the company. If you reject the goods in this manner, the HP company must refund the payments you have made.

If you do not want to reject the goods, but would like, for example, a free repair, you should write to the company, explaining what is wrong with the goods and that you would like a free repair.

You are also entitled to claim compensation for any expenses you incur which were reasonably foreseeable by both you and the company at the time you entered the HP agreement; for example, if you bought a car on HP and it proved faulty, the cost of alternative means of transport while the car was being repaired would be an allowable expense.

Once you have paid all the instalments on your goods, your consumer rights become the same as if you had paid cash.

Banking

When you open a bank or building society account you are making a contract, and all the usual rules governing contracts to supply a service apply, including the stipulation that the bank or building society must carry out the contract with reasonable skill and care.

A banking code of practice, 'Good Banking', aims at improving your rights and the service you are offered by banks and building societies. It includes provisions relating to the following:

- **fair conduct** – banks and building societies should always act 'fairly and reasonably' in dealings with customers
- **a ban on 'charges on charges'** – if your current account goes into the red purely because of the charges that have been taken from it, you should not incur a second lot of charges
- **plastic cards** – for any type of plastic card, credit card, bank card and so on, the maximum liability for money taken without your agreement is £50, or nil if the card is lost or stolen before it reaches you. You will lose this protection only if you've been 'grossly negligent' by, for example, writing your Personal Identification Number (PIN) on the card – and it is up to the bank or building society to prove that this is the case
- **confidentiality** – your personal financial details *won't* be passed to separate 'non-banking' companies in the banking group – such as their insurance or investment arm – without your consent. In

practice, this probably means that new customers wil be given a straight 'yes/no' choice of whether to give their consent, and existing customers (who are deemed to have agreed to this sharing of information) will be given the right to object

- **complaints** – all institutions must set up proper internal complaints procedures.

Banks and building societies are starting to adhere to the spirit of the Code, but there are still problems which need addressing. For example, banks still need to do more to inform customers about bank charges and interest rate charges.

In most cases, problems with financial matters can be resolved by a letter to the relevant branch manager or area manager. If this proves unsatisfactory, take your complaint further by writing to the head office, then to the appropriate ombudsman. The Banking Ombudsman Scheme includes all the major banks and all types of bank business normally conducted through their branches. Note that awards recommended by the Ombudsman of up to £100,000 are only binding on banks, not on consumers. (See Addresses at the back of this book.)

The Building Societies Ombudsman covers all societies and can recommend awards of up to £100,000.

Unauthorised withdrawals

If a cashpoint withdrawal appears on your account statement which you suspect is due to a technical problem with the cash dispenser machine, write to your bank or building society. The bank will need to know whether you had your Personal Identification Number written down; whether there is any possibility that another person (even a member of your family) may have borrowed your card and whether there is any chance that you had forgotten about a visit to a cash dispenser, since the date that appears on your statement is not always the same as the date when you withdrew the cash. If your branch is not prepared to settle the matter to your satisfaction, it is worth taking your claim to its head office and then to the appropriate Ombudsman.

Direct debit problems

A standing order is an instruction you give to your bank or building society authorising it to pay a specific amount of money at regular intervals to another person or organisation. In other words, it is instructed to initiate payments from your account. You can pay by standing order to anyone who has a bank or building society account. If you want to change the amount of a standing order, you have to issue a new instruction to your bank to that effect.

With a direct debit, you give your bank or building society the authority to debit your account with payments requested by payee with whom you agree payment terms by completing a direct debit form or 'mandate'; you instruct your bank or building society to permit a payee to draw on your account; the payee ('direct debit originator') initiates payment by asking your bank to release money from your account – your bank only allows the payee to draw on your funds.

Bank and building societies thus delegate responsibility for initiating payments to payees. Because control of the amount and timing of the payment is in the hands of the originator, every originator must be relied upon to operate the system properly. Unlike payees of a standing order, a payee can ask for payment by direct debit only if approved by the banks and building societies who run the direct debiting scheme.

Ultimately the banks and building societies guarantee that customers paying by direct debit do not suffer from originators' mistakes; they reimburse customers if a direct debit which does not conform to the customer's instructions is charged to the customer's account.

Stolen cheques

If your cheque book is stolen, you are not liable for any fraud provided you let your bank or building society know of the theft as soon as possible. But fraud using cheques that you have already written is another matter.

Unless you write out cheques using specific wording (see below), a thief can fake the signature of the person to whom you are paying the money (the 'payee') on the back of a cheque you have already written out, even if you have crossed it, pay it into his own account and, when it clears, withdraw the money and disappear. In these circumstances, you would have no redress against either the bank where the cheque was paid in or your own bank which paid the cheque. The problem is that virtually all cheques are transferrable. The two parallel lines simply mean that the cheque has to be paid through a bank account.

However, the Cheques Act 1992 states that if you write the words *'Account Payee'* or *'a/c payee'* with or without the word *'only'* on the face of a crossed cheque, you are protected against the cheque being transferred to a thief's account. If the bank where the cheque is paid in negligently credits an account other than that of the payee named on the face of the cheque, it will have to make good the payer's loss.

Investments

The Financial Services Act 1986 (FSA) regulates all providers of investment products or advice. This covers products such as personal pensions and endowment policies, but it does not cover mortgage lending, deposit savings (such as TESSAs) or medical insurance. Under the Act, investment salespeople and advisers are required to give consumers 'best advice', taking account of their personal details and circumstances. The 'know your customer' rule, for example, means an adviser must gather enough information about a consumer's circumstances to put the adviser in a position to assess needs and decide upon the appropriateness and suitability of products.

Similarly, the rules under the FSA control the way products can be marketed – for example, any illustrations or projections should be based on standard assumed rates of return so that consumers are not given misleadingly optimistic figures.

Complaints about breaches of FSA rules are made to the relevant regulatory body, such as the Personal Investment Authority (PIA) for Independent Financial Advisors (IFAs) or the Insurance Ombudsman Bureau for insurers. These bodies have powers to award compensation when things go wrong. Alternatively, a consumer who has lost out because of bad advice could start court action.

Accountants

Legally anyone can call themselves 'an accountant' but there can be a huge difference between the services offered by an unqualified person and those offered by a qualified professional. Chartered accountants, for example, undergo lengthy training and are required to maintain standards of professional conduct and competence supervised by the Institute of Chartered Accountants in England and Wales (or its sister bodies in Scotland and Ireland).

The range of services offered by accountants covers auditing, financial reporting, taxation, personal finance, corporate finance, financial management and information technology. To find a firm, first try personal recommendations. If you want a full list of chartered accountants practising in your area, contact the Institute. Draw up a short list and then ask whether they have experience in your field, what range of services they can offer, how fees are charged and so on.

When you instruct an accountant, you are entitled to have the work done with reasonable skill and care. This is laid down by the Supply of Goods and Services Act 1982. The accountant should also follow your instructions and any professional guidance and standards in the area. If giving investment advice (see page 153), the accountant must comply with all the relevant rules and regulations under the Financial Services Act 1986.

The Institute will take up complaints against members and has a disciplinary procedure. Otherwise, you may have to go to court to get redress. This may be complex and expensive so get legal advice before proceeding.

Rejecting a credit company's offer of a rebate on early settlement

Dear

[Reference: account number]

I am writing in response to your letter of **[date]** containing an offer of a rebate on the above credit agreement, taken out on **[date]**, which is regulated by the Consumer Credit Act 1974.

Under the Act, I have the right to pay off the outstanding debt at any time, having given notice to you of my intention to do so. I am legally entitled to a rebate on early settlement and, after giving notice, I am required to pay off the outstanding debt less the correctly calculated rebate.

As you are no doubt aware, the rebate is calculated by reference to a table set out in the Rebate in Early Settlement Regulations. In my particular case, I am entitled to a rebate of approximately **[£.....]**. Your offer of **[£.....]** falls short of the statutory amount and you are under a legal obligation to provide me with a further reduction in the debt.

If I do not receive your proposals for a further reduction within 14 days of the date of this letter, I shall have no alternative but to pursue the matter further.

Yours sincerely

Rejecting a credit company's demands for excessive increases in repayment

Dear

[Reference: account number]

I write in response to your letter of **[date]** informing me that the APR for my credit agreement has been increased from **[..... per cent]** to **[..... per cent]**.

At the time of entering into the agreement, you assured me in full knowledge of my financial circumstances that although the APR was variable, it was unlikely that it would be increased beyond the **[..... per cent]** you were quoting. The above increase means that my monthly payments have now been increased from **[£.....]** to **[£.....]**.

The type of agreement that I have entered into with you is regulated by the Consumer Credit Act 1974. The fact that you have raised the APR on my agreement to an unacceptable level means that the agreement is extortionate as defined by the terms of Sections 137–40 of the Act.

I urge you to reconsider the unreasonable interest charge you have imposed and to reduce the APR to its original level or, alternatively, a reasonable level. If I do not receive your proposals for a reduction in the interest charge within 14 days, I shall have no alternative but to submit this matter to the adjudication of the county court without further reference to you.

Yours sincerely

Claiming a refund from a credit card company on a purchase from a bankrupt supplier

Dear

[Reference: account number]

On **[date]** I ordered **[item]** from **[retailer]** at a cost of **[£.....]** and for which I paid using my **[describe]** credit card. I have paid the relevant credit card bill covering this purchase.

The **[item]** has not been delivered, despite letters to the supplier dated **[dates]** and I have discovered that the supplier has gone into liquidation.

I understand that under Section 75 of the Consumer Credit Act 1974 the credit card company is liable to the customer for any breach of contract or misrepresentation along with the supplier of goods and services.

The **[supplier's]** failure to deliver the **[item]** is a breach of our contract, and as I paid by credit card I hold you liable for this breach. I therefore expect you to credit my account with the full purchase price of **[£.....]** within the next 14 days. If you fail to reimburse me I shall have no alternative but to issue a summons against you in the county court for recovery of the money without further reference to you.

Yours sincerely

NOTE
If the credit card company does not settle your claim, take it to court using the small claims procedure (see Chapter 17).

Querying erroneous charges on a credit card statement

Dear

[Reference: account number]

I have received the current statement of this account, which contains charges for purchases that I have not made. The charge's reference is **[number]**, the supplier **[name]**, the amount **[£.....]** and its date is **[date]**.

I have not made any purchases from this supplier. As I have neither lost my card nor revealed to anybody my card number, I believe that I am a victim of a credit card fraud.

Please look into this matter without delay and send me copies of the voucher allegedly bearing my signature. If the purchase was made by telephone, please send me details of the transaction.

In the meantime, I am enclosing a cheque in respect of my outstanding bill less the sum of the disputed transaction. While this matter is being sorted out, I expect the disputed charge to be removed from my account, so that it does not incur interest.

I look forward to hearing from you within the next 14 days.

Yours sincerely

encs.

Asking a credit card company to waive its fee

Dear

[Reference: account number]

I am currently reviewing my financial arrangements and am considering switching to one of the many credit cards with no annual fee and a lower interest rate.

I have been pleased with my card and would like to keep it if possible. However, there are now several cards with similar benefits (such as purchase protection insurance) to your card but are cheaper.

If I am to stay with your company, I would therefore want to waive the annual fee that I would otherwise be charged. If you are not prepared to do this, I shall have no alternative but to close my account with you and switch to another card issuer.

I would be grateful if you could let me know your position as soon as possible. I look forward to hearing from you.

Yours sincerely

Rejecting faulty goods bought on HP

Dear

[Reference: credit agreement number]

I acquired **[item]** on **[date]** from **[supplier]** under a hire-purchase agreement with you. The **[item]** has developed serious defects **[describe in detail]**.

In accordance with my rights under the Supply of Goods (Implied Terms) Act 1973, and my right to reject under common law, I now terminate my hire-purchase agreement with you on the grounds that the **[item]** was not of satisfactory quality when purchased.

I call on you to take back the **[item]**, and to refund all sums which I have paid to you under the agreement. These sums include the deposit and the instalments paid since the agreement was entered into, making a total paid of **[£.....]**. In addition I am claiming compensation for the expenses, inconvenience and loss of use of the **[item]** due to the above defects.

In my view of the serious nature of the above defects, I am not prepared to consider any proposition that further attempts be made to repair the **[item]**, nor shall I be paying any further instalments.

I am therefore ceasing to pay any further instalments.

Please let me know when you intend to collect the **[goods]** and to refund all the payments I have made.

Yours sincerely

Informing a bank's/building society's head office of unauthorised cashpoint withdrawals

Dear

[Reference: account number]

I am enclosing copies of my correspondence with your **[location]** branch, where my account is held.

As you will see, an unauthorised withdrawal has been made from my account from a **[details: type of dispenser, date, time]**. I could not have made this withdrawal because at the time I am supposed to have used the card I was elsewhere **[details]**. My Personal Identification Number (PIN) is not written down and I have not revealed it to anyone. Nor has my cashpoint card been lent to anyone.

I therefore maintain that these debits are not in any way the result of my actions, and are due to some defect in the procedure for processing cash card debits and withdrawals. Accordingly I expect to receive a revised statement within the next 14 days.

Yours sincerely

encs.

NOTE
If you do not receive a satisfactory response write to the relevant Ombudsman.

Complaining to a bank/building society about bank charges

Dear

[Reference: account number]

I have received the current statement of this account, which shows that you have made a charge of [£.....].

The charge was for a bounced cheque. However, my account is always in credit and I have not written any cheques that have bounced.

In any event, the Banking Code of Practice recommends that banks and building societies introduce systems that ensure that consumers are given at least 14 days' notice of charges to be deducted from an account. Since you have failed to give such notice, you have failed to follow the Code.

I enclose a copy of the statement detailing the charge, and expect to receive a refund of [£.....] plus any loss of interest within the next 14 days.

Yours sincerely

Complaining to a bank/building society about errors in the execution of a direct debit instruction

Dear

[Reference: account number(s)]

I have two accounts at your branch. One is in joint names **[specify account name and number]**; the above account is in my name alone.

There are no direct debits in respect of my account but a direct debit has been arranged in respect of the joint account. **[Details; payee]**.

Sums have been released from the wrong account, **[details]** resulting in an overdraft on the above account, for which I am now being charged.

On **[date]**, I was told that you were not liable for this and that it was the payee's responsibility to sort out the problem.

In order that I may clarify the situation, please let me have a copy of the direct debit instruction so that I may ascertain that all its details are correct.

I look forward to hearing from you within 14 days.

Yours sincerely

Rejecting a bank's/building society's denial of liability for the incorrect execution of a direct debit instruction

Dear

[Reference: account number]

Thank you for your letter of **[date]** enclosing a copy of the direct debit instruction made out in connection with **[payee]**.

The instruction was made out correctly, but you have made the following error in carrying it out **[details].** Since the error is clearly yours I am not prepared to pay the relevant charges currently set against my account **[details]**.

I expect you to sort out the matter to my satisfaction within the next 14 days. If you do not, I shall take the matter up with the ombudsman **[specify]**.

Yours sincerely

Requesting information on the use of a credit reference agency when an application for credit is rejected

Dear

[Reference: credit application number]

Thank you for your letter of **[date]** rejecting my application for credit **[details]**.

I cannot understand why my application has been turned down, and would like to know whether a credit reference agency has been used in considering my application. If this is the case, please give me its name and address so that, in accordance with my rights under the terms of Sections 157–60 of the Consumer Credit Act 1974, I may write to the agency concerned to ascertain whether the information it supplied to you is correct.

I look forward to hearing from you in due course.

Yours sincerely

Complaining about information supplied by a credit reference agency and asking for reconsideration of an application for credit

Dear

[Reference: credit application number]

I recently applied for your credit card under the above reference and my application was turned down. Your letter of **[date]** indicated that this was due to adverse information supplied to you by **[name]** credit reference agency.

I wrote to the agency to obtain a copy of my file and was surprised to find the following record **[describe]**. This matter has nothing to do with me. I therefore wrote to the agency again on **[date]** asking it to amend my file. The agency has agreed to do this.

In the circumstances, I would like you to reconsider my application, and look forward to hearing from you within the next 14 days.

Yours sincerely

Complaining to a bank about encashment of a stolen cheque

Dear

[Reference: account number]

On **[date]** I wrote a cheque **[number of cheque]** for **[amount]** payable to **[name]**, adding the word 'only' after the payee's name and the amount. I also crossed out the printed words 'or order' and wrote 'Account payee' between the two printed parallel lines.

The cheque was posted to **[payee's name]** on **[date]** but was intercepted by a thief who, I understand, wrote **[payee's name]** on the back of the cheque, so that it seemed that **[payee's name]** had authorised the transfer of the money to the thief. Having endorsed the cheque in this way, the thief paid it into his own account and, when it cleared, withdrew the money.

Since I made out the cheque to **[payee's name]** only and wrote 'Account payee' between the parallel lines, the cheque should have been paid into the payee's account only. In accordance with the Cheques Act 1992 the cheque was not transferrable but was valid only between **[payee's name]** and myself.

As the cheque was not credited to the account of **[payee's name]** I am legally entitled to be reimbursed, and I therefore look forward to receiving your cheque for **[amount]** within seven days.

Yours sincerely

Asking the Banking Ombudsman/Building Societies Ombudsman to intervene in a dispute with a bank

Dear

[Reference: bank/society and account number]

I am in dispute with the above **[bank/society]** in respect of unauthorised withdrawals made from my current account.

I am enclosing all the relevant correspondence, from which you will see that I have been unable to reach a settlement with **[branch]**, despite having contacted its head office.

I would therefore be grateful if you would consider the case on my behalf.

Yours sincerely

encs.

Complaining about bad advice from an investment adviser

Dear

[Reference: product type and reference number]

I am writing to you to complain about the above product.

When I first talked to you on **[date]**, I made it clear that my circumstances were as follows **[describe]**.

I was led to believe that I was taking out a product that was appropriate to my needs. When I received my annual statement on **[date]** I discovered that the product did not meet my requirements as follows **[describe problems]**.

Under the Financial Services Act 1986 you are required to give consumers 'best advice', taking account of their personal details and circumstances.

The fact that the above product does not meet my requirements clearly shows that you have failed to give best advice. I therefore expect to receive compensation from you covering the difference between what I will get from the product and what I would have earned had you given best advice and advised me to take out a more appropriate product. I calculate this to be **[£.....]**.

Under the Financial Services Act 1986 you are required to deal with this complaint. I therefore look forward to hearing from you within the next 14 days. If this matter is not resolved to my satisfaction, I will refer it to the Personal Investment Authority Ombudsman Bureau.

Yours sincerely

Complaining about an inappropriate endowment policy

Dear

[Reference: policy number]

I am writing to you to complain about the above endowment policy I took out with your company on **[date]**.

When I took out the policy I was led to believe that I was taking out a **[number of years]** with-profit endowment policy. When I received my annual statement on **[date]** I discovered that the policy was a whole-life policy.

When I first talked to your adviser, I made it clear that I wanted the following **[describe product]**. As you have failed to carry out my requirements, I expect to receive a refund of the premiums paid, plus interest within the next 14 days.

Under the Financial Services Act 1986 you are required to deal with this complaint. If this matter is not resolved to my satisfaction, I will refer it to the Personal Investment Authority Ombudsman Bureau.

Yours sincerely

Complaining about bad pension advice

Dear

[Reference: product type and reference number]

I am writing to you to complain about the above product you advised me to take out with **[company]** on **[date]**.

As you will know from your records, your firm advised me to transfer benefits from the pension scheme offered by my employer **[name]** and buy a personal pension scheme instead. Following this advice I entered into the pension plan mentioned above.

I understand that all investment firms who sold personal pensions between 29 April 1988 and 30 June 1994 are reviewing these sales to find out whether consumers were badly advised and suffered financial loss as a result.

I believe that you failed to give me 'best advice', taking account of my personal details and circumstances. I therefore expect to receive compensation from you covering the difference between what I will get from the product and what I would have earned had you given best advice and advised me to take out a more appropriate product.

Under the Financial Services Act 1986 you are required to deal with this complaint. If I do not hear from you within the next 14 days, I will refer it to the Personal Investment Authority.

Yours sincerely

Asking the PIA Ombudsman to intervene in a dispute with a member company

Dear

[Reference: investment company and policy number]

I am in dispute with the above investment company, which I understand is a member of your scheme.

I have been unable to reach a settlement with the company in respect of **[describe complaint]**. I am therefore referring the matter to you.

I enclose copies of all the relevant correspondence, and I look forward to hearing from you in due course.

Yours sincerely

encs.

Complaining to an accountant about unsatisfactory work

Dear

I am writing to complain about the service you provided when I instructed you to prepare the following **[describe]**.

When I first spoke to you on **[date]** and showed you my files, I made it clear that my circumstances were as follows **[describe]**. It has now become apparent from **[source]** that the advice you gave me and the accounts you subsequently prepared on my behalf are deficient in the following respects **[describe]**.

The Supply of Goods and Services Act 1982 requires you to carry out your service as an accountant with reasonable skill and care. The problems described above show that you failed in your legal obligations. I therefore have a claim against you for breach of contract.

Because of your breach of contract I have suffered the following loss **[describe]**.

I consider that **[£.....]** would be a reasonable sum of compensation for your failure to meet your legal obligations. I therefore look forward to receiving your cheque within the next 14 days.

Yours sincerely

Asking the Institute of Chartered Accountants to intervene in a dispute with an accountant

Dear

[Reference: name of firm of accountants]

I am in dispute with the above named accountants concerning the service I received from the firm on **[date]**.

I enclose copies of the relevant correspondence. As you will see, the service I received from the firm caused me to suffer the following loss **[describe]**.

I contacted the accountants on **[date]** to complain about this matter but the dispute has not been resolved to my satisfaction.

Since the accountant involved is a Chartered Accountant I am now referring the matter to you for investigation. I look forward to hearing from you in due course.

Yours sincerely

encs.

Chapter 11

Insurance

Claiming on your insurance policy

This section tells you how to claim on the main types of insurance policies held by consumers: home insurance (buildings and contents), holiday insurance and car insurance.

To make your claim, contact your insurance company (or broker, if you are insured with Lloyds) as soon as possible, stating your policy number and brief details of your claim. You will then get a claim form which you must complete and return, normally within 30 days.

On receipt of the claim, your insurance company may arrange for a loss adjuster to visit you to assess whether your claim is valid; it may pay the claim in full, or it may make an offer of less than the sum claimed.

Loss adjusters are independent of insurance companies and Lloyds' underwriters, and are hired to investigate and advise on claims on their behalf. You can in turn appoint a loss assessor who will charge a fee for representing you. The loss adjuster will ask you a number of questions to establish the validity of the claim and will then make a report to the insurer, which usually includes a settlement figure. If you are not satisfied by the insurance company's offer, write again explaining why you are dissatisfied.

If you have exhausted the insurance company's complaints procedure (set out in your insurance policy) and your claim has not been settled, contact the Insurance Ombudsman (see Addresses at the back of this book).

Membership of the Ombudsman scheme is voluntary, but it covers most insurance companies, and deals with the unfair treatment of customers by member companies, poor service and maladministration. You usually have six months from the time you reach deadlock with the insurer in which to make a complaint. Awards recommended by the ombudsman are currently binding on companies up to £100,000 (or £10,000 a year in permanent health insurance cases), although claims for more than this can be considered. Awards are not binding on complainants, so if you are not happy with the outcome you can still go to court later. Check whether your insurer belongs to the scheme before taking out a policy – if it does not, your only hope of redress may be to go to court.

Claiming on buildings insurance

An insurance policy is not a maintenance contract. It is intended to provide cover for specific damage or loss – fire, storm or whatever – *not* to pay for your running repairs. It is a condition of buildings insurance that you keep your property in good condition and take reasonable steps to avoid damage to it.

If your insurance company is not prepared to settle your claim you will have to prove the validity of your claim. To succeed with a claim for storm damage, for example, you will have to prove that the property was damaged as a result of a violent wind accompanied by rain. You will need evidence backing your claim, so if you feel there is the slightest chance that your claim may be disputed, take photographs of the damage as soon after it occurred as possible and ask the repairer to give you a written report detailing the work that has been done to remedy the problem. You will also need evidence from the Meteorological Office that there was a storm. If you do not provide this kind of evidence, it may be very difficult to prove your claim.

Claiming on contents insurance

Home contents insurance covers your household possessions, but only against certain eventualities such as theft. If your property has been stolen, you must report the theft to the police at once. If you do not, your insurance company could refuse to meet your claim. Check the wording of your policy to see how much to claim. If your policy offers 'new for old' cover, you are entitled to claim the cost of new items to replace those destroyed or stolen; with indemnity cover you claim the cost of replacing the item less an allowance for wear and tear.

If a thief broke into your house and damaged a door or smashed windows, for example, you could claim for the damage to the structure of the property on your buildings insurance. If the incident has damaged both the structure of your home and its contents and you have buildings and contents insured with the same insurer, you need complete only one claim form and the claim will be processed as one. If your buildings and contents insurance are with different insurers, you will have to make two separate claims.

If you are claiming for something that has been damaged but can be repaired – a scratched table, for example – claim the cost of repairs. You will need to get two or three estimates and then get the repairs carried out for the lowest price.

If you are dissatisfied by the insurance company's offer, try to get evidence, such as receipts and independent valuations, to back your claim.

Claiming on holiday insurance

Lots of things can go wrong with holidays, so it pays to take out comprehensive insurance when you book. Read the terms of your policy carefully, and if you have to claim make sure you follow the procedures set out in it. Do not rely on a telephone call; make your claim in writing, and keep a copy.

The minimum cover you need will depend on your personal circumstances and your destination, but for a typical holiday you require the following:

- **medical expenses:** these should cover all reasonable medical, hospital and emergency dental treatment. The minimum cover should be about £250,000 in Europe; £1 million in USA and the rest of the world
- **cancelling or curtailing your holiday:** the circumstances covered should include the illness or death of the insured person, a close relative or business associate, or travelling companion; redundancy; jury service or being called as a witness in a court case; severe damage to the insured person's home by fire, flood

or storm, and burglary or other criminal acts against him which necessitate his presence at home. The minimum cover should be the full cost of the holiday, including the deposit.

- **belongings and money:** at least £1,500 cover should be provided for loss of, or damage to, the insured person's property and currency
- **delayed departure:** look for at least £20 or more after the first 12 hours' delay, and the full cost of the insured person's holiday if he cancels after the first full 24 hours' delay
- **delayed baggage:** if baggage is delayed by 12 hours or more on the outward journey the traveller will need cover to pay for emergency purchases until it arrives. The minimum cover you should look for is £75
- **personal liability:** if the insured person accidentally injures someone or damages someone's property, he might be legally liable to pay compensation. Look for cover of £1 million.

If you have to claim you must get all the evidence before you return home, so keep all relevant receipts and bills. Take a copy of your policy with you on holiday so you know the exact extent of your cover.

If you have to cancel your holiday

Most holiday insurance policies cover cancellation and give details of the circumstances in which insurers will pay. Almost all policies cover those insured against inability to travel owing to illness or the illness of a close relative. Check the wording of your policy.

Claiming on car insurance

You are obliged by law to have car insurance. The legal minimum you need covers claims made against you for personal injury to other people (including passengers) and their emergency medical expenses, damage to other people's property caused by you, and limited legal expenses. Most consumers want a more comprehensive policy than this and choose 'third party' cover. This gives the legal minimum cover extended to all public and private roads, plus cover for damage and injury to other people caused by your passengers. One step up from this is 'third party, fire and theft', which provides third party cover, plus cover in the event of your car and/or property fitted to it (such as the radio) being stolen or damaged by lightning, fire and explosion, or of the car being damaged during theft or attempted theft. This kind of cover does not include the contents of the car – a briefcase, sports bag etc. that might be in it. If you do not want to end up paying for your own repairs should your car be damaged, and you cannot prove that the damage was the other driver's fault, you need comprehensive insurance. This gives you the components of 'third party, fire and theft' cover, plus cover for damage to, and theft of, your car, and its contents (often up to £100), your medical expenses (often up to £100) and the cost of taking your car to a garage then home again after an accident.

Motorists often complain that the settlement offered by an insurance company is less than they feel the car is worth. Normally, the value of the car is taken as its market value at the time of the theft or damage being sustained.

If you are unhappy with the offer you receive, you will have to prove that the car is worth more than the sum offered. The sort of evidence that might help would be invoices for work or items which you consider must have enhanced the car's value.

If your car is written off following an accident but not totally destroyed, it may be possible to challenge the insurance company's offer by obtaining a report on the value of the car at the time of the accident from an independent assessor. The Institute of Automotive Engineer Assessors (see Address at the back of this book) will give you the name of an assessor in your area. If you are a member of a motoring organisation such as the RAC or AA, ask that organisation to help with your claim.

Road accidents

If your vehicle is involved in an accident and you do not have comprehensive insurance, you will have to claim your losses from the driver of the other vehicle involved. Even if you are covered, you will usually have uninsured losses, such as any excess you have to pay on your own policy; loss of no-claims discount; compensation for personal injuries; loss of earnings; damaged clothes or other personal items; and the reasonable cost of alternative transport.

You will be able to claim only if the collision was caused by the other driver's negligence — for example, because the other driver did not look where he was going. You would not be able to claim if no one was to blame for the collision.

With some comprehensive policies, your insurer will try to recover your uninsured losses on your behalf from the other driver. If you are trying to claim them back yourself, write to the other driver setting out the details of your claim. Although your legal rights to compensation are strictly speaking against the other driver, insurance companies will often step in, so you could find that you are dealing with the other driver's insurer.

Informing an insurance company of a claim on buildings insurance

Dear

[Reference: policy number]

I write to confirm our telephone conversation of **[date]**.

At **[time]** on **[date]** this property sustained serious damage **[describe]** due to **[circumstances]**. As it was an emergency I called in **[appropriate professional]**, who carried out temporary repairs. This work cost [£.....].

I wish to claim for the cost of the temporary repairs **[describe]** and for the eventual cost of remedying the damage as follows **[describe]**. Please send me the appropriate claim form.

Yours sincerely

Rejecting an insurance company's denial of liability

Dear

[Reference: policy number]

Thank you for your letter of **[date]**, in which you rejected my claim against the above policy for **[damage]** on the grounds that **[reason]**.

I refute your arguments on the basis of the wording of the policy, **[quote wording]**. Furthermore, I enclose a report from a relevant expert, backing up my claim as follows **[details of report]**.

This shows that the damage was caused by **[cause]** and was not in any way due to **[neglect etc.]** as you suggest. I am therefore covered by the terms of this policy, and expect you to reimburse me the sum of **[£.....]** as detailed in my original claim of **[date]** within 14 days.

Yours sincerely

encs.

Rejecting an insurance company's continued denial of liability

Dear

[Reference: policy number]

Thank you for your letter of **[date]** rejecting my claim for **[£.....]** following the damage to this property that occurred on **[date]**.

I maintain that the damage was caused by **[circumstances]** and should therefore be covered by the above policy. Prior to **[date of damage]** the property was well maintained and in good repair, as is proved by **[proof – tradesmen's invoices etc.]**, therefore lack of proper maintenance could not have contributed to the damage.

I now ask you to reconsider my claim in light of this evidence, and look forward to receiving your cheque in settlement of my claim within 14 days.

Yours sincerely

encs.

Final letter to an insurance company in a dispute over building insurance

Dear

[Reference: policy number]

On **[date]** I claimed on this policy for **[describe damage]**, which occurred on **[date]**.

Although you have written to me on several occasions denying liability, I feel that I have presented sufficient evidence to you in the form of **[describe]** to prove that my claim is covered by the policy.

It is now **[.....]** weeks/months since my claim was submitted and I feel that you have taken far too long to deal with this matter. Unless I receive your proposals for settlement within 14 days, I shall put the matter in the hands of the Insurance Ombudsman Bureau.

Yours sincerely

NOTE
If your claim is not settled following this letter write to the Insurance Ombudsman Bureau (see Addresses at the back of this book).

Rejecting an insurance company's offer on a claim

Dear

[Reference: policy number]

Thank you for your letter of **[date]**, offering only **[£.....]** in respect of the **[item]** which was **[details of loss/damage]** on **[date]**.

Since receiving your offer I have found a valuation certificate made by **[valuer]** dated **[date]** valuing the **[item]** at **[£.....]**. In the light of this valuation, a copy of which is enclosed, I feel that your offer is too low and ask you to reconsider my claim.

I look forward to receiving your revised offer within 14 days.

Yours sincerely

encs.

Informing an insurance company of a claim on holiday insurance

Dear

[Reference: policy number]

I wish to make a claim on the above holiday insurance policy.

I have just returned from holiday **[dates, location]**. On **[date]** my **[item]**, worth **[£.....]**, was **[reason for claim: theft, damage etc.]**. I reported the matter to the police in **[place]** on the day of the occurrence and have written confirmation of this. Please send me the appropriate claim form.

I look forward to hearing from you in due course.

Yours sincerely

Informing an insurance company of a claim for a cancelled holiday

Dear

[Reference: policy number]

On **[date]** I booked a holiday **[describe: dates, location etc.]** with **[tour operator]**.

I am now unable to take this holiday because **[details of medical or other valid problem]**. As a result, I am left with no alternative but to cancel my holiday, and have therefore written to the tour operator to this effect.

In the circumstances I am making a claim on my travel insurance policy, which covers me for the full cost of the holiday in the event of cancellation or curtailment due to illness or injury.

I look forward to hearing from you in due course. If there is any other information that you need to process my claim please let me know.

Yours sincerely

NOTE
You may have to prove that the illness or other problem is serious enough to make you unable to travel. This will certainly involve getting medical or other evidence, so ask your GP or other professional to provide a report backing up your claim.

Rejecting an insurance company's offer following a claim on car insurance

Dear

[Reference: policy number]

Thank you for your letter of **[date]**, in which you offered me **[£.....]** in respect of the damage **[describe]** to my vehicle **[make, model, engine capacity]** as a result of **[circumstances causing damage]** on **[date]**.

Since receiving your offer I have obtained an independent valuation of my car from **[organisation/garage]** to the effect that the market value of the car at the time of the above incident was **[£.....]**. A copy of the report is enclosed.

In the light of this evidence I am not prepared to accept your offer, and I expect you to reconsider it, taking the above valuation into consideration. I look forward to hearing from you within 14 days.

Yours sincerely

encs.

Claiming compensation for damage to a vehicle caused by a negligent driver

Dear

[Reference: accident and registration numbers of both vehicles]

The collision which occurred between the above vehicles at **[time, date]** at **[location]** and which was caused, as you admitted, by your negligence and through no fault of my own, resulted in **[damage: describe]** to my vehicle.

I have made a claim for the above damage under my comprehensive insurance policy, but as a result of your negligence and your failure to notify your insurers of the accident I have incurred costs for uninsured losses **[details]** totalling **[£.....]**.

I hold you directly responsible for these expenses and I am legally entitled to receive compensation from you. I therefore expect to receive your cheque for **[£.....]** within 14 days.

Yours sincerely

NOTE
If the other driver does not reply to this letter or does not offer satisfactory compensation, send another letter threatening court action (see overleaf).

Threatening a negligent driver with court action

Dear

[Reference: accident and registration number of both vehicles]

I have not received a reply to my letter of **[date]** and now write to inform you that, unless I receive your satisfactory proposals for settlement of my outstanding claim within seven days of the date of this letter, I shall have no alternative but to issue a summons against you in the county court for recovery of the money without further reference to you.

Yours sincerely

Asking the Insurance Ombudsman Bureau to intervene in a dispute with an insurance company

Dear

[Reference: insurance company and policy number]

I am in dispute with the above insurance company, which I understand is a member of your scheme.

I have been unable to reach a settlement with the insurance company in respect of an offer it made in connection with **[item]** following my claim of **[date]**. I am therefore referring the matter to you for investigation.

I enclose copies of all the relevant correspondence, and I look forward to hearing from you in due course.

Yours sincerely

encs.

Chapter 12

Solicitors

WHENEVER you instruct a solicitor to act on your behalf, you are making a contract. The contract has certain terms, the most obvious of which are that the solicitor will do the work – the conveyancing of your house, say – and that you will pay for that work.

What to ask a solicitor

- **How much do you charge?** Solicitors charge for their services generally on an hourly rate. Rates can vary as there is no uniform way of calculating them. Solicitors' charges are based on factors like the type of work being done, the solicitors' expertise and experience, the speed at which you need advice and where the firm is based. Find out the firm's hourly rate before you seek legal advice from them. Solicitors are now free to advertise their rates, but few choose to do so.
- **How many hours' work are likely to be involved?** Get a written estimate and set a ceiling on the costs.
- **What other costs might be involved?** It may be necessary to use a barrister or to get expert evidence.
- **When will I have to pay?** Get a clear timetable of payment.
- **What are you going to do next and what is the timescale involved?**
- **Would you confirm the advice given in writing? And what do I need to do next?**

The final reckoning

Unfortunately the final bill may be much more than the original estimate. It is risky taking a case to court – even if you win, you may have to pay some of your own fees. You may have to accept less than you claimed because of the risks involved in proceeding after an offer has been made. And if you lose, you might have to pay the other side's costs as well. All these factors should be considered when contemplating whether to use a solicitor.

It is not possible to calculate a solicitor's fees exactly as there is no set scale of charges. However, it is implied into the contract between both parties that the solicitor's bill must be fair and reasonable.

If you are unhappy with the bill you receive for 'contentious work' (that is, where court proceedings have been started), you should request a detailed breakdown of the bill. The solicitor is obliged to provide you with this under Section 64 of the Solicitors' Act 1974. To challenge the bill further, you can apply for the costs to be 'taxed' in court. This means that a special bill is drawn up and the court decides whether each item is fair and reasonable.

A word of warning – 'taxation' as defined above can be expensive. Not only will you have to pay a fee to the court to have the bill taxed, but, if the bill is reduced by less than one-fifth, you will lose the court fee and have to pay the solicitor's costs of going to court as well as your own.

If you feel that a bill for 'non-contentious work' (where the case being handled by the solicitor does not involve court proceedings) is too high, ask the solicitor involved for a detailed breakdown of the charges. If, having received a detailed breakdown, you still feel the bill is too high, ask the solicitor to apply to the Law Society for a Remuneration Certificate. This states whether the solicitor's bill is fair and reasonable and, if it is not, suggests another reasonable sum. If you feel that the certified amount is still too high, you still have the right to apply for the costs to be 'taxed' by the court.

The procedure for complaints about solicitors' charges in Scotland is broadly similar to that in England and Wales. However, there is no statutory right to a detailed breakdown of the bill and system of Remuneration Certificates. So regardless of court proceedings, if you wish to challenge a solicitor's bill, you must require him to have it taxed. This is done by the Auditor of Court. Otherwise complain to the Law Society of Scotland arguing that overcharging amounts to incompetent work (see below).

Incompetent work

If you have a complaint about the way your solicitor is handling your case, you should first try to resolve the problem with the firm. Under professional practice rules solicitors must have a procedure for handling complaints. Your solicitor should have told you, when you first instructed the firm, whom to contact with a complaint. If you have not been given a name, write to the Complaints Handling Partner.

If you believe that your solicitor's work is incompetent or 'shoddy', to use the correct term, you can complain to the Office for the Supervision of Solicitors (OSS) (see Addresses at the back of this book). The range of problems the Office investigates includes delay in answering your letters or failing to answer them at all; delay in dealing with your case; failing to deal with your money properly; deception; failing to hand over your papers at your request when you are not in debt to the solicitor, and any substandard work which may have caused you inconvenience or distress, but has not caused you a financial loss for which you could sue.

Once you have complained to the Office it will investigate your claim and contact the solicitor on your behalf in an effort to resolve the problems you are experiencing. If appropriate, the Office can take disciplinary action against the solicitor. The Office also has powers to award compensation of up to £1,000. The Law Society of Scotland (see Addresses at the back of this book) has broadly similar powers.

In addition, the Legal Services Ombudsman oversees the way in which complaints against solicitors (and barristers and licensed conveyancers) are handled by the appropriate professional bodies. Before you contact the ombudsman you must have exhausted the complaints procedure of the OSS. If you have done so, and are not satisfied with the handling of your complaint or the decision reached, you can then ask the Ombudsman to investigate on your behalf (see Addresses at the back of this book). There is no limit on the amount of compensation that may be awarded by the Ombudsman, but awards are not strictly binding. You must complain within three months. In Scotland, you should contact the Legal Services Ombudsman for Scotland (see Addresses at the back of this book).

Claiming for negligence

If you claim that your solicitor has been negligent, and you want financial compensation, you may have to take the claim to court. Get advice on your legal position from another solicitor, preferably one with experience of negligence work. If you cannot find an appropriate solicitor to help you, the OSS will put you in touch with a member of the Law Society's Negligence Panel, who will give you up to an hour's free advice. If you decide to proceed, you can ask that solicitor to take on your case. In Scotland, if you cannot find a solicitor to act for you, the Law Society of Scotland will appoint a solicitor (called a 'troubleshooter').

In England and Wales, if your claim does not exceed £3,000 your case would normally be dealt with under the small claims procedure in the county court. If you want to claim more than this, there will be a full hearing in the county court. In Scotland, claims up to £750 are heard under the small claims procedure of the Sheriff Court. Claims over £750 but under £1,500 are heard under the summary procedure.

Asking a solicitor for a breakdown of a bill

Dear

[Reference: invoice number]

Thank you for your letter of **[date]** containing your invoice for **[£.....]**.

As you know, we have not been able to reach agreement on the sum that I should pay you for the **[service]** you did on my behalf.

So that I can get a clearer understanding of the component parts of your bill, I would be grateful if you would provide me with a detailed breakdown of all the items involved. I am entitled to this under Section 64 of the Solicitors Act 1974.

I look forward to hearing from you within 14 days.

Yours sincerely

Asking a solicitor to obtain a Law Society Remuneration Certificate

Dear

[Reference: invoice number]

Thank you for your letter of **[date]** containing a detailed breakdown of the work undertaken on my behalf and the costs accruing to it.

I am still not satisfied with the amount that I am expected to pay for the **[service]** undertaken on my behalf.

I am legally entitled to instruct you to obtain from the Remuneration Certificate department of the Law Society a Remuneration Certificate stating what, in the Society's opinion, is a fair and reasonable charge for the work done. I would be grateful if you would now do so.

I look forward to hearing from you within 14 days.

Yours sincerely

Paying under protest while a solicitor obtains a Remuneration Certificate

Dear

[Reference: invoice number]

On **[date]** I asked you to apply to the Law Society for a Remuneration Certificate.

I am concerned that if your account remains unpaid you will charge me interest. To avoid that eventuality, I enclose a cheque for the full amount of your bill. This payment is made on the strict understanding that it is subject to the outstanding application for a Remuneration Certificate continuing and that I will be appropriately reimbursed should the Certificate state that your bill should have been lower. If you do not agree to this condition, please return my cheque.

Yours sincerely

encs.

NOTE
Solicitors do have the right to charge interest on unpaid bills, hence the need to pay under protest to avoid subsequent interest charges on whatever fee is finally agreed upon.

Complaining about the slowness of a solicitor's conveyancing

Dear

[Reference: account number or similar]

I instructed you to undertake **[service]** on my behalf on **[date]** and I am becoming increasingly concerned about the amount of time you are taking in the fulfilment of that service. I would therefore be grateful if you would clarify in writing the following points:

(a) why the matter has taken so long to get to its current stage

(b) what is left to be done and how long it should take

(c) what you estimate the costs incurred so far to be.

I look forward to hearing from you within the next 14 days.

Yours sincerely

Asking the Office for the Supervision of Solicitors to intervene in a dispute with a solicitor

Dear

[Reference: name of solicitor]

I would be grateful if you would consider my complaint about shoddy work by the above-mentioned firm of solicitors, whom I instructed on **[date]** to perform **[service]** on my behalf.

I enclose copies of all the relevant correspondence together with my own diary of events relating to the problem. The gist of my complaint is that the above solicitor's work has proved substandard in the following way: **[problem in detail]**. I understand that you may send copies of these documents to the solicitor concerned. If you require any further information, please contact me.

I look forward to hearing from you in due course.

Yours sincerely

encs.

Complaining to the Ombudsman about the Office for the Supervision of Solicitors (OSS)'s handling of your claim

Dear

[Reference: name and address of solicitors]

I am writing to you about my dispute with the above firm of solicitors in respect of **[describe]**.

On **[date]** I sent my file of papers to the Office for the Supervision of Solicitors and asked it to intervene. On **[date]** the Office contacted me saying that it was unable to resolve my complaint to my satisfaction for the following reasons **[describe]**.

I do not regard the Office's response as satisfactory because **[describe]**. I am therefore referring the matter to you for investigation.

I enclose copies of all the relevant papers, and I look forward to hearing from you in due course.

Yours sincerely

encs.

Chapter 13

Health

IF YOU have a complaint about the services or treatment you receive from the NHS – whether it is from a hospital, GP, optician, pharmacist or dentist – and you want an apology and explanation you should refer the matter directly to the person involved. This procedure is known as local resolution and it should be possible to resolve the problem in this way. Talk to the doctor, nurse or whoever else is involved about what happened and explain what you would like done about it. If you would prefer to talk to someone who was not involved in your care, write to the complaints manager at the NHS trust (or health authority if your complaint is about a family practitioner such as a GP or dentist). The address will be in the phone book.

You have to make your complaint within six months of the problem coming to your notice. If you complain about a family practitioner then the staff in the surgery or the complaints manager in the health authority will probably investigate. They may need to look at records and meet you to gather the facts. You can expect to get an acknowledgement of your complaint within two days and a full written response within ten working days. You have the right to a written reply from the chief executive within 20 working days if your complaint is about a trust or health authority.

If you are not satisfied with the response, you can request an independent review but this must be done within 28 calendar days of the written reply to your complaint. The response should tell you who to contact. Your request will be considered by a specially trained member of the trust or health authority – the convener – who will ask you to explain in writing exactly why you are still dissatisfied. The convener will decide within 20 working days (or ten if you are complaining about a family practitioner) whether or not to set up an independent review panel. If it is set up, they will write to you to tell you which matters the panel will investigate. The panel will fully re-examine your complaint and a final report will be sent to you and the other people involved. The chief executive of the trust or health authority will write to inform you of any action to be taken.

If you are still dissatisfied after the NHS complaints procedure has been completed you can ask the Ombudsman (known as the health service commissioner) to investigate your case. He is independent of the NHS and the government and his services are free. As well as complaints about NHS services, he can investigate complaints about how the complaints procedure is working if, for example, you want to appeal against a refusal to set up an independent review panel. You must appeal to the Ombudsman in writing within a year of the event. If the Ombudsman decides to take on your case, he will undertake a thorough investigation and make recommendations to the relevant NHS bodies. He will often refer the case back to the convener for reconsideration. The Ombudsman will not generally take on a case which has not first been through the NHS complaints procedure, or a case which is being dealt with by the courts. If you have any doubt as to whether the Ombudsman can deal with your complaint, contact his office beforehand.

If you think an NHS or private health professional has behaved unethically or unprofessionally (e.g. drunkenness or indecency) you can complain to the professional body with which he or she is registered: the General Medical Council for doctors, the General Dental Council or the General Optical Council. Addresses for these are given at the back of the book.

Finally, if you want to claim financial compensation you will probably need to take legal action and prove negligence in court. It is vital in these circumstances to get advice from a lawyer who specialises in this area. Action for Victims of Medical Accidents (a national charity) can put you in touch with a solicitor and support groups.

For complaints about private medical treatment your only option is to take the matter up yourself with the practitioner concerned. If you cannot get a satisfactory response and you wish to claim compensation you may have to consider court action.

An NHS charter for patients

The Patient's Charter 1995 sets out patients' rights and NHS standards. Your rights are:

- to be registered with a GP
- to change your GP quickly and easily if you wish
- to receive information on local health services, including what to expect and maximum waiting times
- in virtually all cases to be guaranteed admission for treatment by a specific date no more than two years after being put on a waiting list by a consultant
- to receive information from your GP about the services provided and to see on request the practice leaflet
- to receive a health check on joining a practice, if you have not seen a GP in the last three years, or yearly if you are over 75
- to have any proposed treatment clearly explained – including any risks and alternatives – before you decide whether to have it
- to be referred to a consultant or for a second opinion (but only when your GP agrees)
- to have access to your health records
- to be able to opt out of medical research or student training
- to have any complaints investigated and get a quick, full, written response.

The national standards set out in the Charter include aims covering respect for privacy, dignity and personal beliefs; all emergency ambulances should arrive within 14 minutes in urban areas and 19 minutes in rural areas; at hospital casualty departments patients should be assessed immediately; and out-patients should have a specific time for an appointment and be seen within 30 minutes of it.

You may obtain a copy of the charter from Patient's Charter, Freepost, London SE99 7XU.

Medical records

Both the *Patient's Charter* and the Access to Health Records Act 1990 entitle you to see your paper medical records written on or after 1 November 1991. To do so, send a written request to the holder of the record (your GP or dentist, for example), or, in the case of hospital records, the local health authority (health board in Scotland and Northern Ireland). The holder must give you access to your records within 40 days; you can choose either to go to see the records or be sent a copy. You get access free if your records have been added to in the last 40 days (in practice, if you have been treated during this time). If your records have not been amended recently, you can be charged up to £10. If you think the record is incorrect, you will have to ask for it to be put right. If the holder disagrees with you, a note of your views must be put on your file.

Remember, though, that you have no right of access to information recorded before the start date of 1 November 1991. The only way you will be able to see previously recorded paper records is if the holder of the records – your GP, for example – is willing to show you on an informal basis.

Complaining to your Health Authority about a doctor's conduct

Dear

[Reference: doctor's name and practice]

I wish to complain about the quality of service I have received from the deputising service of the above GP.

At **[time]** on **[date]** I telephoned the deputising service and asked them to send a GP as quickly as possible for the following reason **[describe]**. However, the doctor was **[.....]** hours late and his behaviour was unsatisfactory in the following way **[describe]**. I was dissatisfied with his diagnosis and undertook to organise **[the patient's]** admittance to hospital **[name]**, where he was diagnosed as **[describe]** by **[second doctor]**. The **[patient]** was subsequently given treatment for this condition **[describe]**. The behaviour of **[initial doctor]** was unacceptable and I would be grateful if you would investigate his conduct.

I look forward to hearing from you in due course.

Yours sincerely

Requesting an independent review

Dear

I am writing further to the letter of **[date]**, which I received from my **[doctor's surgery/local health authority/local NHS trust]** concerning my complaint about **[doctor]**.

They have investigated my complaint but I am not satisfied with their response. I consider that my complaint is very serious. It is clear to me that the doctor was in breach of **[his/her]** professional terms of service in that **[describe nature of events]**. I therefore wish to pursue my complaint further.

I understand that you have been appointed as the convener in this case, and would be grateful if you would consider my request for an independent review panel to be convened to investigate my complaint.

I look forward to hearing from you in due course.

Yours sincerely

Complaining to your Health Authority about a dentist's charges

Dear

[Reference: dentist's name and address of practice]

I am writing to you to complain about the above dentist's charges.

On **[date]** I visited his surgery for the first time. After an examination he told me I needed **[describe treatment]** and I agreed to have National Health treatment. When this was completed I was presented with a bill for **[£.....]**, a copy of which is enclosed. This was unacceptably high.

When I questioned it, **[dentist]** told me his reasons **[describe]** which I found unacceptable, and so I refused to pay the bill. Subsequent events **[describe]** left me no alternative but to pay the bill in full under protest.

I am dissatisfied with the outcome of this matter and I would ask you to look into this matter on my behalf.

I look forward to hearing from you in due course.

Yours sincerely

Complaining to the General Dental Council about a dentist's behaviour

Dear

[Reference: dentist's name and address of practice]

I wish to complain about the behaviour of the above dentist.

When I attended his surgery at **[time]** on **[date]**, his behaviour was unprofessional **[describe]**. As a consequence of this behaviour, I felt unable to go through with the appointment and promptly left the surgery.

I would therefore be grateful if you would investigate the conduct of **[dentist]**.

Yours sincerely

Complaining to an optician about unacceptable service

Dear

[Reference: make and model of spectacles]

On **[date]** I attended an appointment for an eye test.
You then prescribed lenses, and I selected suitable frames.

When I collected the spectacles I complained that the
lenses were not consistent with those selected as a result
of my eye test **[describe problem]**. Despite your
assurances to the contrary, the problem persisted. I
subsequently visited your shop on **[date]** but was told
that you were not prepared to replace the spectacles, nor
were you prepared to adjust them.

The Supply of Goods and Services Act 1982 requires
you to carry out your services with reasonable skill and
care. It also requires you to use materials of satisfactory
quality and reasonably fit for their purpose.

The problem outlined above shows that you have failed
to fulfil these legal obligations and I have a claim against
you for breach of contract. However, I am prepared to
give you an opportunity to undertake the necessary
remedial work to bring the spectacles to a reasonable
standard within a reasonable time.

I expect you to do this within 14 days. If you fail to do
so, I shall have no alternative but to retain another
optician to put the matter right and look to you to bear
the cost of the work, as I am legally entitled to do.

Yours sincerely

Requesting access to medical records

Dear

[Reference: record holder's name and practice]

I would like to see my medical records. I understand that I am entitled under the Access to Health Records Act 1990 to see paper medical records concerning me that were written on or after 1 November 1991, and that the Data Protection Act 1984 entitles me to see medical records relating to me that are held on computer.

My medical records will have been updated within the last 40 days as a result of treatment I received from you on **[date]** for **[describe]**. I am therefore entitled to access to my records free of charge, and I would like a copy of then sent to me direct.

Although I have no right of access to information recorded on paper before 1 November 1991, I would also like to see a copy of previously recorded paper records. I hope that you are willing to show me these records on an informal basis, and I look forward to hearing from you shortly.

Yours sincerely

Complaining to an NHS Trust hospital's complaints manager about a long wait on the waiting list

Dear

I am writing to you to complain about the amount of time I have had to wait for treatment for my condition **[describe]**.

On **[date]** my GP **[name and address of practice]** wrote to **[name of the specialist]** referring me to the specialist for treatment. The specialist first saw me as an outpatient at your hospital on **[date]** and decided that it was necessary to admit me to hospital. I was therefore put on the appropriate waiting list. However, I am still waiting to be admitted to the hospital for treatment.

Under the Patient's Charter I am entitled to be admitted for treatment by a specific date no later than 18 months from the date the specialist put me on the waiting list. It is now later than that. You have therefore failed to meet the standard set out in the Charter.

As you can appreciate, I am anxious to be treated and so expect you to fix an appointment for my admission to hospital straightaway. I therefore look forward to hearing from you within the next seven days.

Yours sincerely

Complaining to an NHS Trust hospital's complaints manager about poor outpatient treatment

Dear

I am writing to you to complain about the amount of time I have had to wait for treatment from your outpatients' clinic.

On **[date]** my GP **[name and address of practice]** wrote to **[name of specialist]** referring me to the specialist for treatment for my condition **[describe]**. On **[date]** the hospital wrote to me confirming an appointment on **[date and time]**. Although I arrived at the clinic in good time, I was ignored for a considerable amount of time. When I asked what was happening I was told that the specialist could not see me until **[time]**. When I complained about the long delay, I was given no explanation or apology.

Under the Patient's Charter the specialist was required to see me within 30 minutes of the time of my appointment. The fact that I had to wait **[time]** shows that you failed to meet the standard set out in the Charter.

Since the delay was considerable, I would like you to look into this matter and explain what happened.

I look forward to hearing from you in due course.

Yours sincerely

Complaining to an NHS Trust hospital's complaints manager about a postponed operation

Dear

I am writing to you to complain about the postponement of my scheduled operation for my condition **[describe]**.

As you will know from your records, my operation was scheduled to take place on **[date]**. However, when I arrived at the hospital on that day I was told that my operation had been cancelled because **[describe circumstances]**. I was also told that you would contact me to fix another date for the operation.

As you can appreciate, the late cancellation of the operation has caused me considerable inconvenience and distress. Under the Patient's Charter you should not have cancelled my operation on the day I was due to arrive at the hospital.

I am anxious that the operation should take place soon and so expect you to fix another appointment straightaway. I therefore look forward to hearing from you within the next seven days.

Yours sincerely

Chapter 14

Neighbours

WHATEVER kind of problem you are experiencing with your neighbours, first try to sort it out amicably with them. If a reasonable direct approach does not work, take formal action. You will need evidence substantiating your claim, so keep a detailed diary of each incident or disturbance.

As a householder, you have certain rights over your property; similarly your neighbours have such rights over their property. At times, these rights may clash. This is when you can call upon the law to step in so that the dispute may be resolved, particularly if you are faced with what is defined as a nuisance – see below.

If you are faced with a nuisance caused by neighbours and you have failed to settle your differences, you can in some circumstances complain to your local council, who may prosecute your neighbour under criminal law. Alternatively, you might take action yourself under civil law.

A word of warning, though: behaviour that annoys you need not be a nuisance in the legal sense, and so you need to be sure that you really have a case. Strictly speaking, 'nuisance' means unlawful interference with someone else's enjoyment of their own land. Bear in mind, too, that civil cases can be very expensive, so before embarking on court action you should consult a solicitor.

Noisy neighbours

If you are bothered by noisy neighbours, contact the Environmental Health Department of your local authority. You will have to satisfy them that the noise is unreasonably loud, is disturbing your sleep or is interfering with your enjoyment of your property, and so amounts to a legally defined nuisance. After investigation, the council may serve a notice on the neighbours forbidding the playing of loud music, say, or limiting it to certain times or to more reasonable levels. If your neighbours continue, they risk a fine of up to £2,000 – plus a further £50 for every day that the nuisance continues unabated.

Alternatively, instead of approaching the local authority, you can go direct to the Magistrates' Court (Sheriff Court in Scotland). Again, you will need evidence, and will have a better chance of success if you get statements from other neighbours, or even a doctor's note saying the noise is affecting your health. Your neighbours may be fined if the noise continues.

You can seek an injunction (an interdict in Scotland) in the county or High Court (Sheriff Court in Scotland) forbidding the neighbour to continue the disturbance. The advantage of this is that you can also claim compensation for the annoyance and disturbance you have suffered. But the procedure can be very expensive, so you should consult a solicitor before applying for an injunction.

Also, the Noise Act 1996 gives local authorities additional powers to deal with loud noise coming from domestic premises between 11pm and 7am. The Act creates a new night-time criminal offence: offenders are now liable to £100 on-the-spot fines; hi-fi equipment, say, can be confiscated; and there is a maximum £1,000 fine in cases that come to court. Councils in England and Wales can use the new law at their discretion to tackle noise problems. Complaints should be made to your local environmental health department. If poor insulation is to blame, the environmental health officer can serve a notice on the property owner demanding improvements.

Bonfires

Whether bonfires constitute a legally defined nuisance depends on whether they interfere with anyone's use and enjoyment of their own property, and whether the bonfires are lit more frequently than an ordinary person would consider reasonable. Occasional bonfires, such as the burning of unwanted mail and circulars once a week, may not constitute a nuisance. But if you consider someone's frequent bonfires unreasonable, keep a detailed diary of when they are lit and get statements from other people affected by them.

If you cannot persuade your neighbour to be more reasonable, contact your local Environmental Health Department. It can serve a notice on your neighbour requiring the lighting of the fires to stop (though this is unlikely), or to occur less frequently, or even requiring the site of the bonfires to be moved to a different area of the garden. If your neighbour ignores the notice, the local authority could take him or her to the magistrates' court. If found guilty, your neighbour would be liable to a fine, fixed by the court, of up to £2,000 plus a daily penalty, currently £50, if he or she continues causing a nuisance.

You can bypass the local authority and go straight to the magistrates' court yourself to ask for a 'nuisance order'. This is similar, in effect, to the action taken by the local authority. But remember that you will have to prove your case, so make sure that you have evidence supporting your case: a diary of events, other neighbours' statements and so on.

Overhanging branches

You are legally entitled to cut off any branches overhanging your property at the point where they cross the boundary. Technically you must offer them back to your neighbour, as the branches remain his or her property. (This applies equally to any fruit trees whose fruit-laden branches dangle temptingly over the garden fence.)

A word of warning: the tree may be subject to a Tree Preservation Order, so before you start lopping check with your local authority. If the tree is protected, you will need consent from the appropriate authority before you do any cutting. And if you live in a Conservation Area, you should ask the local authority before you start lopping the tree: the authority has six weeks in which to decide whether or not to issue a Tree Preservation Order.

If cutting the branches was intended to increase light to your property, but fails to do so, there may be very little else you can do. You do not have a right to light; you can acquire a right to light by express agreement with your neighbour (which is unusual) or by long usage – because you have received a certain level of light for at least 20 uninterrupted years, say. But this applies only to particular windows in your home, never to gardens. Even then, you have no redress if it is a natural object like a tree that is blocking the light.

Root problems

If the roots of a neighbour's trees cause any damage to your property, your neighbour is liable, and you can claim compensation, by suing in court if necessary (see Chapter 17). The neighbour cannot avoid liability just because the tree was there before you occupied the house.

If the tree's roots have caused subsidence to your property, you will probably be covered for this damage by your building insurance; it is far simpler to make a claim under the policy than to sue your neighbour.

Neighbours' short cuts

Each time they walk across your garden, your neighbours are trespassing, unless you have invited them on to your property. If a friendly word does not stop your neighbours doing this, you are perfectly entitled to bar their way, in person if need be. If faced with repeated acts of trespass, you may apply to the county court (Sheriff Court in Scotland) to get an injunction (interdict in Scotland). You will need advice from a solicitor before doing this.

Moreover, if the neighbours cause damage to your property while trespassing, you can claim compensation. The size of your claim will depend on the number of times your neighbours have trespassed on your garden; the distress and inconvenience it has caused you and whether your garden has been damaged. Damage to your prize flower-bed, for example, would give you a claim for greater compensation than if you were simply complaining about someone trespassing on your concrete drive. Keep a log of events and take photographs of any damage.

Complaining to a neighbour about noise

Dear

On **[date]** I was disturbed by unacceptable levels of noise in the form of **[describe]** coming from your house.

When I asked you to reduce the level of noise, your behaviour was unacceptable **[describe]**. The **[nuisance]** continued **[describe circumstances]** causing **[effect on writer]**. This has occurred on **[.....]** occasions over the past **[period]**.

I am therefore writing to let you know that I am unable to tolerate any further disturbance. If I am disturbed by **[nuisance]** once more, I will have no alternative but to sue you for compensation in the county court. I will also apply for an injunction restraining you from making a similar amount of noise in the future.

Yours sincerely

Complaining to the Environmental Health Officer about a nuisance caused by a neighbour

Dear

I am writing to complain about a nuisance caused by my neighbour **[name]** of **[address]**.

My complaint is as follows **[describe nuisance in detail]**. On **[.....]** occasions I have asked my neighbour to desist, but he refuses to do so.

This level of disturbance is unacceptable to me. I am considering taking a civil action against my neighbour but before I embark on that course I would appreciate your help with this matter.

I look forward to hearing from you in due course.

Yours sincerely

Complaining to a neighbour about bonfires

Dear

You have lit a bonfire in your garden on **[.....]** occasions during the last **[period]** and the resultant smoke adversely affects my enjoyment of my property as follows **[describe effects]**.

I have repeatedly asked you to stop making these fires, but you ignore my requests. I have therefore consulted a solicitor, who advises me that the bonfires are lit more frequently than would generally be considered reasonable and that their interference with my enjoyment of my property constitutes a public nuisance.

If you do not stop lighting the fires I will report the matter to the Environmental Health Department.

Yours sincerely

Informing a neighbour of an intention to prune an overhanging tree

Dear

I am writing to let you know that the branches of your [.....] tree which overhang my property cause the following problem [describe].

Would you please let me know if the tree is, to your knowledge, protected by a Tree Preservation Order. If it is not, I shall exercise my legal right to cut off all the branches overhanging my property.

I look forward to hearing from you within the next 14 days.

Yours sincerely

Complaining to a neighbour about damage caused by tree roots

Dear

During the last **[period of time]** I have noticed the following problem **[describe]**, which was caused by the roots of the trees **[describe]** in your garden. An independent surveyor's report has confirmed that these roots are to blame and I enclose a copy of that report.

You are legally responsible for the damage to my property.

Please let me know within the next 14 days whether you are prepared to repair the damage, which you are welcome to inspect in advance. If not, I will have the work done by my own contractor and will look to you to pay the cost of the repair in full, as I am legally entitled to do.

Yours sincerely

enc.

Complaining to a neighbour about acts of trespass

Dear

I initially complained to you about trespass on **[date]**, and since then I have told you on a great many occasions that I do not want **[persons involved]** to trespass on my property. Nevertheless you persist in **[describe]**.

If you continue to commit this **[act of trespass]** I shall, in accordance with my legal rights, apply to the county court for an injunction restraining **[persons involved]** from so doing. I shall also put in a claim for the considerable distress and inconvenience which you have caused me.

Yours sincerely

Chapter 15

Local authorities

THE structure of local government is complex. If you have a problem that falls within the remit of your local authority, first identify which department in the authority is responsible. Look in your phone book (local authorities often have whole pages devoted to their service) or find out from your local library, Citizens Advice Bureau, council officer or councillor 'surgery' (usually published in your local paper).

Before writing to complain, phone the relevant department and ask for the name of the official who would be dealing with your query. Alternatively, address your letter to the director of whichever department you need, such as the Director of Highways. (Writing to the director will get your letter to the right person in the end but not necessary as quickly as you would like.)

If you are not satisfied with the service you receive from your local authority, ask whether there is a Citizen's Charter covering the department in question and ask for it to be sent to you. Many authorities have published service commitments; if yours has, it should state the standard of service you are entitled to expect. If your problem is still unresolved, ask for a copy of the complaints procedure (particularly if you have received poor personal treatment). It can also pay to see a local councillor at this stage. Finally, if you are still not getting anywhere, contact your Local Government Ombudsman (the Ombudsmen deal with complaints about poor administration). If the Ombudsman finds that you have suffered an injustice because of poor administration, the report of the Ombudsman's investigation will contain a recommendation on the action the Ombudsman expects the local authority to take.

Planning matters

Planning permission is intended to make sure a proposed development fits in with the locality. Local planning authorities administer day-to-day planning. Contact the planning department of your local authority to find out what the relevant planning body is for a particular proposal. In Northern Ireland it will be the Department of the Environment (N. Ireland). (At central government level, planning is the responsibility of various Secretaries of State. For example, the Transport Secretary deals with motorways and trunk roads in England.)

Generally, applications for planning permission should be made through the Planning Department at your local authority. Contact the relevant department if you are unsure whether or not planning permission is required for any work you intend to carry out on your property.

Also contact the planning authority if you want to object to a planning proposal. Planning departments are required to notify all affected properties when an application is made. However, planning officers' interpretations of this can vary between notifying only next-door neighbours to notifying whole streets. So the first you may hear about a proposal may be through the local press.

There are plenty of cases where residents have managed to fight off planning proposals or get plans changed, but it often takes years of hard work. Even if you are unsuccessful in the end, you may still win concessions, such as environmental improvements that will lessen the impact of the developments.

Injury caused by tripping up on the pavement

If you trip up on the pavement and injure yourself, you may have a claim against the local authority for negligence, but you will have to prove that the pavement was in a state of disrepair and had not been maintained with reasonable skill and care. There are no hard and fast rules about the condition a pavement has to be in to be the cause of a claim. However, your claim will be stronger if the pavement is in a bad state of repair – as a rule of thumb, if paving slabs protrude by more than one inch from the general level of the pavement.

You will be able to claim for any financial losses you incur (cost of repairs to your clothes and time off work, for example) and your personal injury, for which damages could be high (get legal advice from a solicitor).

Contact your local authority to find out the name and position of the appropriate official to whom to complain.

Asking your local authority to introduce road safety measures

Dear

[Reference: name of road]

I am writing to ask you to consider introducing road safety measures, such as a traffic-calming scheme and zebra crossing on the above road.

My reasons for writing to you are as follows: **[set out nature of problems]**. Because of these problems pedestrians who use the road are in danger of being hurt and injured. In particular **[describe specific dangers, such as those faced by young children and the elderly]**.

As you can appreciate from the above, this is a serious problem and I very much hope that your officers are able to consider the options for dealing with it.

A petition from other concerned pedestrians and users of the road is attached.

I look forward to hearing from you in due course.

Yours sincerely

encs.

NOTE
It will pay to get local councillors and the local press involved at an early stage in this sort of campaign.

Asking your local authority to introduce residents-only parking

Dear

[Reference: name of road]

I am writing to ask you to consider introducing residents-only parking on the above road.

My reasons for writing to you are as follows: **[set out nature of problems, highlighting any traffic problems]**. As a result of these problems it is very difficult for residents to park on the road.

A petition from other concerned pedestrians and users of the road is attached.

I look forward to hearing from you in due course.

Yours sincerely

encs.

Complaining about poor refuse collection

Dear

I am writing to complain about the poor refuse service I receive from you.

Although the refuse in my street is supposed to be collected on **[days and times]** it is not. The collectors come only on **[date and times]**. The refuse collectors also leave litter scattered every time they visit the street. This level of service is unacceptable and causes hygiene problems.

I therefore want you to investigate this problem and let me know what action you intend to take to rectify matters.

I look forward to hearing from you in due course.

Yours sincerely

Objecting to a planning application

Dear

[Reference: planning application for name and address of property]

I wish to object to the planning application that has been made by **[name]** in respect of building works that are intended to be carried out at **[address]**.

My objections to the application are as follows: **[detail, highlighting any conflict between the application and other plans for your area; any increase in traffic or noise and so on]**.

I want you to take these objections into consideration when considering the application.

I look forward to hearing from you in due course.

Yours sincerely

NOTE
When objecting to a planning application show as many factual objections as you can. Also get as much support and publicity as possible. Lobby neighbours, local councillors, write to local papers and so on.

Complaining to a local authority about injury caused by an uneven pavement

Dear

On **[date]** I tripped over a paving stone which formed part of the pavement of **[street]** with the following results: **[describe]**.

You are responsible for maintaining the pavements in good order. The condition of the above pavement **[describe]** is clear evidence that you are in breach of your legal responsibilities.

In these circumstances, I am legally entitled to claim compensation from you. As a result of your failure to maintain the pavement properly, I experienced the following **[describe: loss of wages, damage to clothes etc.]**. I therefore claim compensation of **[£.....]** for financial loss plus **[£.....]** compensation for pain and suffering.

I look forward to receiving your cheque for the total amount within 14 days. If you fail to reimburse me I shall have no alternative but to issue a summons against you in the county court for recovery of the money without further reference to you.

Yours sincerely

Complaining to a local authority about its handling of your problem

Dear

[Reference: nature of problem]

I am writing to complain about your handling of my problem **[describe]**.

As you will recall from your files, I first contacted you on **[date]** to complain about **[describe]**. Since then I have been in lengthy correspondence with you concerning the problem. On **[date]** you wrote to me saying that my complaint could not be resolved to my satisfaction for the following reasons **[describe]**.

I do not regard your response as satisfactory because **[describe, including any breach of charter standards]**. I am therefore referring the matter to you for your reconsideration.

If within 14 days you have not made a reasonable offer to settle my claim, I shall have no alternative but to refer the matter to the Local Government Ombudsman for **[area]**.

Yours sincerely

encs.

Complaining to a Local Government Ombudsman about a local authority's handling of your problem

Dear

[Reference: name of local authority]

I am writing to you about my dispute with the above local authority in respect of **[describe]**.

As you will see from the enclosed file of papers, I have the following problem with my local authority **[describe]**.

On **[date]** I wrote to the director of **[department]** asking for my case to be reconsidered. On **[date]** the director contacted me saying that my complaint could not be resolved to my satisfaction for the following reasons **[describe]**.

I do not regard the local authority's response as satisfactory **[describe]**. I am therefore referring the matter to you for investigation.

I enclose copies of all the relevant papers, and I look forward to hearing from you in due course.

Yours sincerely

encs.

Chapter 16

Other problems

Cancelling a sales agreement made at home

The Consumer Protection (Cancellation of Contracts Concluded away from Business Premises) Regulations 1987 gives you a seven-day cooling-off period during which you have the right to cancel a contract which is made during an 'unsolicited visit' by a salesman to your home. An 'unsolicited visit' means that you have not expressly requested the salesman to call: that includes appointments made as a result of unrequested telephone calls or after delivery of a card proposing a visit. If you initiated the salesman's visit, you are not protected by the Regulations.

The Regulations currently apply to most cash and credit contracts over £35, but do not cover agreements for the sale of food and drink, or other goods supplied by regular roundsmen.

The salesman must give you a notice of your cancellation rights at the time the agreement or offer is made. If he does not, the contract is null and void. You are not penalised for cancelling at any time within the cooling-off period. If you have paid a deposit you can demand its return. To cancel the contract, either send the cancellation notice or write to the trader, saying that you are cancelling the contract in accordance with your legal rights. You must keep the goods safe until they are collected by the trader.

Injury occurring on someone else's premises

If you are injured while on someone else's premises, whether it is a shop, station, office or private residence, you may be able to claim compensation. The occupiers of premises have a legal duty towards you, as laid down by the Occupiers' Liability Act 1957, Act (N.I.) 1957 and Occupiers' Liability (Scotland) Act 1960, to take reasonable care to see that you will be reasonably safe.

You will need to prove that you sustained your injury as a result of negligence on the part of the occupier of the premises. And if the case went to court, it would be left to the judge to decide whether or not the occupier had failed to take reasonable care to see that you were reasonably safe. If for example, while in a shop, you slip on some spilt yoghurt and break your arm, you will have a strong case for compensation, provided the yoghurt had been there long enough for the shop staff to discover it and clean it up, or to put a sign up warning of the danger. If, on the other hand, the yoghurt had just been dropped by a customer and the shop had not had time to cordon off the area or clear up the mess, then you would not be able to prove negligence.

You can claim compensation for the time you have had to take off work, lost wages and the pain and suffering caused by the fall, which could be substantial depending on the seriousness of the injury, and 'loss of amenity'. This means that if you are a painter and decorator, and can not use ladders for six months, for example, you will be entitled to claim more compensation than someone who does not have to climb ladders for a living. Get legal advice from a solicitor on how much to claim.

Junk mail

If you do not want to receive advertising circulars and other forms of junk mail by post, you can write to the Mailing Preference Service (see Addresses at the back of this book) to request that your name and address be removed from mailing lists of companies sending such material. This is a free service set up and funded by the direct mail industry to enable consumers to have the opportunity to have their names and addresses taken off or added to lists used by its members.

If you want to stop unsolicited mail from member companies, write to the MPS for an application form.

Unsolicited goods

If you receive goods that you have not ordered and do not want, sent in the hope that you will buy them, do not worry. The Unsolicited Goods and Services Act 1971, or, in Northern Ireland, the Unsolicited Goods and Services (Northern Ireland) Order 1976, makes this kind of sales technique illegal. Your options under the Act are either:

- to do nothing and keep the goods in a safe place for six months, after which time they become yours to keep. But if the sender wants the goods back during this period, he is entitled to them. You may not refuse to send them back if the sender pays the postage, nor may you refuse to allow him to collect the goods; or:
- to write to the sender giving notice that you did not ask for the goods to be sent, that you do not want them and that they are available for collection by the sender. If the sender does not then collect the goods within 30 days they become your property.

You should ignore all demands on the part of the sender of the goods for payment or to send the goods back, unless the sender pays the postage. You should report the matter to your local trading standards department (in the telephone directory under local authority). Demands for payment in such circumstances are a criminal offence for which the sender may be prosecuted and fined.

Timeshare

The Timeshare Act 1992 provides for a 14-day (minimum) cooling-off period in timeshare contracts signed in the UK. The Act makes it a criminal offence for an operator to enter into a timeshare agreement without first giving you, the customer, notice of your rights to cancel the contract at any time during the cooling-off period. A cancellation form for you to complete and return should be attached to the notice setting out your cancellation rights. If you cancel during the cooling-off period, you are entitled to recover any money you have paid in connection with the contract.

The Act also provides for a minimum cooling-off period of 14 days in the case of most timeshare credit agreements – in other words, where there is a provision for credit with which to pay for the timeshare. As for timeshare agreements, the Act requires provision of a statement, to which a cancellation form should be attached, of your rights to cancel during the cooling-off period. The statement should also set out arrangements for repayment of credit should the agreement be cancelled. In line with other laws covering credit, it is not, however, a criminal offence to fail to hand over a notice of your rights to cancel a timeshare credit agreement.

Unfair small print

The Unfair Terms in Consumer Contracts Regulations 1994 sets out new law on unfair contract terms. The Regulations cover contracts with businesses that were made after 1 July 1995. They add to and do not replace existing protection for consumers, particularly that provided by the Unfair Contract Terms Act 1977 (see page 14).

The Regulations and the 1977 Act say that a consumer is not bound by a standard term in a contract with a seller or supplier if the term is unfair. If a term is 'unfair' it is invalid and will not affect your claim for redress. Only a court can say definitely whether a term is fair or unfair, but the decision would depend on whether:

- the term unduly tips the contract against the consumer and in favour of the business
- that imbalance amounts to a breach of the requirement of 'good faith'.

The Regulations say that businesses must write standard terms in plain and intelligible language.

The Regulations also give the Director General of Fair Trading (at the Office of Fair Trading) powers to stop the use of unfair standard terms by businesses, if necessary by obtaining a court order (an injunction). If you think that any of the standard terms in consumer contracts are unfair, write to the Unfair Contract Terms Unit, Office of Fair Trading (see Addresses at the back of this book). The Unit cannot intervene in an individual case, but your complaint may lead to a change in the contract that the business uses in the future.

Cancelling a contract signed at home

Dear

[Reference: contract number]

On **[date]** one of your salesmen came into my house and asked me to buy **[item]**. I had not asked him to call; his visit was entirely unsolicited. Although I was concerned about signing any documentation, I decided that the only way I could get rid of him was by signing a contract for **[item]**. Under the terms of the contract I paid a deposit of **[£.....]**. I have now decided that I do not want the **[item]**.

I understand that the Consumer Protection (Cancellation of Contracts Concluded away from Business Premises) Regulations 1987 provide for a seven-day cooling-off period, during which consumers have the right to cancel contracts made during an unsolicited visit. I am hereby giving notice that I wish to exercise my rights under the Regulations and cancel my contract with you.

I look forward to having my deposit returned within seven days.

Yours sincerely

Claiming compensation for an accident on someone's premises

Dear

On **[date]** I was on your premises **[shop, office, etc.: address]** when the following accident occurred; **[describe]**.

From the nature of this accident and its cause **[describe: slippery floor, etc.]**, it is clear that your premises were not reasonably safe, and that you had failed to take reasonable precautions to make them so, as you are obliged to do under the terms of the Occupiers' Liability Act 1957. I therefore hold you liable for the accident and the pain and distress I have suffered as a result **[describe if necessary]**.

I am legally entitled to receive compensation from you and I look forward to receiving your proposals for settlement of my claim within the next 14 days.

Yours sincerely

Asking the Mailing Preference Service to remove your name from mailing lists

Dear Sirs

I am inundated with advertisements and other items of unwanted mail, all correctly addressed to me personally at my home.

I understand that I can ask to have my name and address removed from the mailing lists of companies that are members of your service. I therefore request an application form so that I may register that my details be removed from these lists forthwith.

Yours faithfully

Asking the sender of unsolicited goods to arrange for their return

Dear Sir

[Reference: brief description of goods]

On **[date]** I received **[describe goods]** from your firm which I did not order and do not want.

These unsolicited goods are available for collection upon reasonable notice from the above address. Please let me know what arrangements you intend to make for their collection.

Yours faithfully

Cancelling a timeshare agreement

Dear Sir

[Reference: agreement number]

I hereby give notice that I wish to cancel my timeshare agreement.

Yours faithfully

Complaining to the Office of Fair Trading about unfair small print

Dear

[Reference: business name]

I wish to complain about the unfair terms contained in the consumer contract used by the above business.

As you will see from the enclosed copy correspondence, I am in dispute with the business in the following respects: **[describe]**. In response to my claim the business has said that it is not responsible to me because of its standard terms and conditions. In particular, the business has referred me to clause(s) **[number]** of its contract, a copy of which I also attach.

I consider that the terms referred to above are unfair and unreasonable both under the Unfair Contract Terms Act 1977 and the Unfair Terms in Consumer Contracts Regulations 1994.

I understand that you are unable to intervene in this case, but I would ask you to look into this matter with a view to exercising your powers under the Regulations to stop the general use of the unfair standard terms used by this business.

Yours sincerely

encs.

Chapter 17

Going to court

DO NOT be discouraged from pursuing your complaint simply because the other party shows no interest in responding to your letters or causes delays, deliberate or accidental. Threaten to take the matter to court. The purpose of the small claims procedure in the county court is to allow individuals to take their own cases to court. Although you may need help with some of the stages in the procedure, remember that the small claims court uses simplified rules. Below we show how the small claims mechanism works, stage by stage.

When can it be used?

If your claim is for £3,000 or less (England and Wales), your case will automatically be treated as a small claim. Even if it is over this limit, it can be dealt with as a small claim provided the court agrees to this.

Why use it?

Cost is the main advantage to the plaintiff. Even if you lose, the only costs which normally can be awarded against you are those of the defendant's witness and any out-of-pocket expenses. If you win, in addition to any compensation awarded, the court fee (currently between £10 and £70, depending on the amount you are claiming) will be refunded to you, and you can ask to be reimbursed for your own expenses. You do not need a lawyer – this immediately saves you money – because you as plaintiff can easily deal with the appropriate documentation yourself. Free leaflets explaining what to do are available from county courts.

A letter before action

If your complaint is not getting anywhere despite your having followed the guidelines in this book, send a final letter before action threatening to issue a small claims summons. In this letter, you put a time-limit on action by the other party, allowing, for example, seven days in which to send you your refund or compensation.

If your problem is not resolved by this course of action, you may have to issue the summons. But issuing a summons does not necessarily mean that you have to go to court. You can always pull out if the other party pays you or offers a satisfactory compromise. Issuing a summons shows that you mean business and often leads to a sensible offer.

Issuing a summons

Issuing a summons is easy using the small claims procedure. You will need three copies of the appropriate form, N1, a Default Summons – available from your local county court (look under 'Courts' in the telephone directory). One copy is for you, one for the court, and one for the person from whom you are claiming.

You will have to give particulars of your claim. These should set out the basic facts of your case so that the court and the defendant know what the claim is about. Keep the particulars short and to the point.

Send two copies of the form, along with a postal order for the fee to cover the cost of issuing the summons, to any local county court. You will receive a form, N205A, telling you the number of the case. The court will then send a copy of the summons to the defendant.

The defence

Within a couple of weeks of receiving your completed summons, the court sends it to the defendant, who then has 14 days in which to submit a defence. If you do not receive notification of what is happening in this period, check with the court. If a defence is not filed with the court within 14 days of the summons being served on the defendant, you can apply to have judgment given automatically ('in default'). You will need form N14 – Request for Entry of Judgment in Default Action – which is available from the court. Write to the court, enclosing the completed N14 together with the case note sent to you by the court when the summons was issued. Following receipt of these documents, the court will enter judgment in default and return the case note to you saying that judgment has been so entered. You can then take steps to get your money (see below).

If the defendant files a defence, the court will write to you, perhaps informing you that the case has been transferred to another county court if there is one nearer the defendant's home, and that it has been listed for a preliminary hearing (or pre-trial review). Alternatively the court will tell you that the case has been scheduled for a hearing and usually will give you a date when this will take place.

The preliminary hearing

This hearing enables the court and the people involved in the court case to discuss how best to deal with the claim. It also allows you time to try to reach a settlement. If the date proposed for the preliminary hearing is inconvenient, you should write to the court explaining why the date is unsuitable and asking for a fresh date to be fixed. Courts usually agree to such requests.

Exchanging documents

The next step is called discovery of documents. Each side has to prepare a set or list of documents relevant to the case. You should include everything other than privileged documents (these are generally letters between you and your legal adviser). These sets or lists then have to be exchanged with the defendant who in turn has to make a similar set available to you. A standard form to accompany these sets is available from county court offices. Exchanging documents in this way lets you and the defendant know the precise basis of each other's case.

Agreeing directions by letter

If the case is relatively straightforward a preliminary hearing may not be necessary. In this instance you should write to the defendant asking him to agree 'directions for trial' by letter. These directions set out when you will exchange documents and any expert reports you may have, how many expert witnesses you will have, when the trial will take place, and so on. If the defendant agrees to this course of action, send a copy of the agreed directions to the court. If the defendant does not agree to it, you should attend the preliminary hearing.

When your letter proposing the use of 'directions for trial' and the defendant's written agreement to it are received by the court, it will issue a formal set of directions confirming what you have asked for.

You agree when documents are to be exchanged – this is usually within 14 days of the court's formal set of directions. You should also ask the court to set a date for trial and limit the number of experts that each side may call (mechanics submitting evidence about the state of your car, electronics experts giving evidence about your hi-fi, and so on), as this keeps down your expenses. (If you have any experts' reports you should also agree to exchange these at a fixed time – seven days, say, before the hearing.)

Looking at the defendant's documents

When you receive the defendant's list of documents, each document that is not privileged (and therefore has to be disclosed) should be listed and dated: (1) letter to the manufacturer, (2) letter to you, and so on). You should ask to see any documents that you have not already seen, such as letters sent from the defendant to other parties (letters from a shop to its supplier about faulty goods you have bought, for example).

If the case is settled before the hearing

If the case is settled before the hearing, write to the defendant accepting the offer and copy your letter to the court. But do not write to the court saying that the case is concluded until you have received the defendant's cheque.

The hearing

Your case will probably get to final hearing within six months of being set in motion. The hearing takes place in private, before a district judge. District judges differ in their approaches – some ask questions, others simply listen without intervening. You will be asked to present your case. Keep it simple and stick to the particulars you gave when the summons was issued. You will also be asked to call any witnesses you may have (such as an electrical expert, for example, confirming that your new hi-fi is inherently defective). The defendant will then give his side of the story and you will be given the opportunity to ask questions. The defendant may also call witnesses. Once each side has presented his evidence the district judge will give his decision.

The district judge will usually give a judgment there and then. If you win your case, in addition to being awarded all or part of your claim (depending on the judge's decision), you can claim the return of the fee for issuing the summons, together with costs relating to any witnesses, and travel expenses.

Getting your money

Winning the case in court (getting judgment) is one thing; getting your money is another. Once you have won the case you should write to the loser, called the judgment debtor, telling him to pay up within a fixed period – seven days, say. If he does not, you will have to take steps to enforce the judgment. A free booklet, *Enforcing Money Judgments in the County Court*, is available from your local county court and tells you the various steps that are available to you.

Four tips

- Make sure that you are suing the person who is legally responsible for the cause of your complaint – a name on a letterhead, for example, may only be the trading name, not the real registered company.
- Read everything the court sends you very carefully. Court forms and language are not as clear as they could be. If in doubt, ask for help. The court staff or district judge should be able to answer your queries.
- Put your evidence and arguments together carefully and avoid irrelevant elements.
- Keep receipts for all expenses you intend to claim.

Court errors

Complaints about administrative errors in the courts are fairly common. Court staff may have made an error listing your case, they may have mislaid your papers, there may have been delays in issuing court papers, and so on.

People complaining about administrative errors in the courts have some means of redress. These include (depending on the nature of the complaint): lodging appeals within the court structure; judicial review; and writing to the Chief Clerk, or the Court Service (the executive agency which administers most of the court structure).

The Charter for Court Users also now covers consumers' rights. The Charter covers your role as a juror, a witness or defendant in a criminal case in the Crown Court, and has special standards for divorce and family cases. It also lists what you can expect if you have anything to do with the county court (including the small claims court) or the High Court. For example, if you have made a claim in the county court, you can expect:

- to have the case heard in court within 40 days once you have told the court you are ready for trial
- to be sent a copy of the court's decision within 10 days
- have a response to your letters to court within 10 days
- to have any written complaint acknowledged within two working days and a reply within 20 days from the date the court receives your complaint.

Magistrates' courts have their own charters administered by local magistrates' courts committees.

Complaints about bad service (but not the outcome of your case) should be made first to the court's customer service manager. You should make further complaints in writing to the Chief Clerk. If you are not happy with the reply, write to the Courts Administrator. The name and address of both will be displayed in your local court office. If you are still not happy, you can write to the Court Service Customer Service Unit asking for an independent investigation.

As far as bad decisions by judges are concerned, the way in

which you get redress is by appealing against the decision which you think is wrong. Always get legal advice before considering an appeal since the costs involved may be substantial.

If you want to complain about the way a judge personally has treated you in court (apart from the decisions made in your case), you should write to the Judicial Appointments Group. You should give the name of the court, the court case number, the date of the hearings, the name(s) of the judge(s) concerned and the reasons for your complaint.

A 'letter before action'

Dear

[Reference: if any]

Further to my letter of **[date]**, to which you have not replied, I now write to inform you that, unless I receive your satisfactory proposals for settlement of my outstanding claim within seven days of the date of this letter, I intend to issue a summons against you in the county court without further reference to you.

Yours sincerely

County Court Summons (NI)

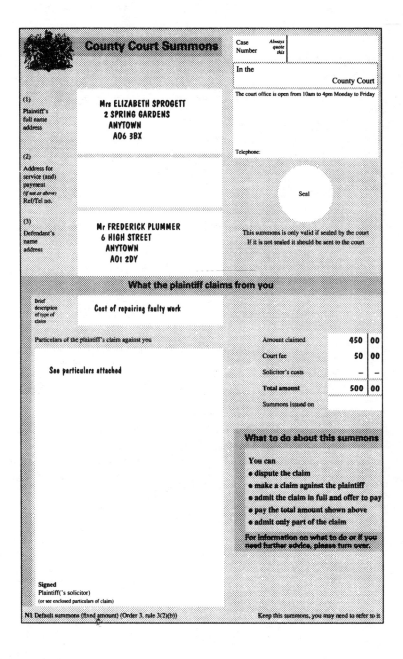

Court Particulars – claiming the cost of repairing faulty work

IN THE **[Name]** COUNTY COURT

Case No. _____

BETWEEN:

[PLAINTIFF'S NAME]　　Plaintiff

AND

[DEFENDANT'S NAME]　　Defendant

_____

PARTICULARS OF CLAIM

_____

1. At all material times the Defendant carried on business as a **[describe business]** at **[address]**.

2. By a contract in writing made between the Plaintiff and the Defendant, contained in or evidenced by the Defendant's estimate dated **[date and reference number]**, the Defendant agreed to **[describe nature of work]** for the sum of **[£.....]**.

3. It was an implied term of the contract that the Defendant would carry out the work with all due care, skill and diligence and in a good and workmanlike manner and with materials which were of a reasonable quality.

4. In breach of the implied term set out in paragraph 3 above, the Defendant failed to carry out the work with all due care, skill and diligence and in a good and workmanlike manner and with materials which were of a reasonable quality.

Particulars of Breach

[Precise details of faulty work]

5. By reason of the matters set out above the Plaintiff has suffered loss and damage.

Particulars of Loss

Cost of remedial work **[£.....]**

AND THE PLAINTIFF CLAIMS:

Damages limited to **[£.....]**

Signed_____ Dated_____

To: The Defendant

　　The District Judge

Court Particulars – claiming the cost of repairing faulty goods

Case No. _____

IN THE **[Name]** COUNTY COURT

BETWEEN:

[PLAINTIFF'S NAME]   Plaintiff

AND

[DEFENDANT'S NAME]   Defendant

PARTICULARS OF CLAIM

1. At all material times the Defendant carried on business as a **[describe business]** at **[address]**.

2. By a contract in writing made between the Plaintiff and the Defendant, contained in or evidenced by the Defendant's estimate dated **[date and reference number]**, the Defendant agreed to supply the Plaintiff with a **[describe goods]** for the sum of **[£.....]**.

3. It was an implied term of the contract that the goods should be of merchantable quality.

4. In breach of the implied term set out in paragraph 3 above, the goods were not of merchantable quality.

Particulars of Breach

[Precise details of faults in goods]

5. By reason of the matters set out above the Plaintiff has suffered loss and damage.

Particulars of Loss

Cost of repairs to goods **[£.....]**

AND THE PLAINTIFF CLAIMS:

Damages limited to **[£.....]**

Signed _____ Dated _____

To: The Defendant

The District Judge

Notice of issue of Default Summons (N205A)

Notice of Issue of Default Summons - fixed amount

To the plaintiff ('s solicitor)

> MRS E SPROGETT
> 2 SPRING GARDENS
> ANYTOWN
> A06 3BX

Your summons was issued today. The defendant has 14 days from the date of service to reply to the summons. If the date of postal service is not shown on this form you will be sent a separate notice of service (Form N222).
The defendant may either

- **Pay you your total claim.**
- **Dispute the whole claim.** The court will send you a copy of the defence and tell you what to do next.
- **Admit that all the money is owed.** The defendant will send you form of admission N9A. You may then ask the court to send the defendant an order to pay you the money owed by completing the request for judgment below and returning it to the court.
- **Admit that only part of your claim is owed.** The court will send you a copy of the reply and tell you what to do next.
- **Not reply at all.** You should wait 14 days from the date of service. You may then ask the court to send the defendant an order to pay you the money owed by completing the request for judgment below and returning it to the court.

In the	ANYTOWN	County Court
The court office at	**COURT BUILDINGS**	
	6, WEST STREET, ANYTOWN	
is open between 10am & 4 pm Monday to Friday		
Tel:		
Case Number *Always quote this*		**98/16254**
Plaintiff *(including ref.)*		**MRS E SPROGETT**
Defendants	**MR FREDERICK PLUMMER**	
Issue date		**22/7/98**
Date of postal service		**31/7/98**
Issue fee	£	**50.00**

For further information please turn over

Request for Judgment

- Tick and complete either A or B Make sure that all the case details are given and that the judgment details at C are completed. Remember to sign and date the form. Your signature certifies that the information you have given is correct.
- If the defendant has given an address on the form of admission to which correspondence should be sent, which is different from the address shown on the summons, you will need to tell the court.

A ☐ **The defendant has not replied to my summons**
Complete all the judgment details at C. Decide how and when you want the defendant to pay. You can ask for the judgment to be paid by instalments or in one payment.

B ☐ **The defendant admits that all the money is owed**
Tick only **one** box below and return the completed slip to the court.

☐ **I accept the defendant's proposal for payment**
Complete all the judgment details at C. Say how the defendant intends to pay. The court will send the defendant an order to pay. You will also be sent a copy.

☐ **The defendant has not made any proposal for payment**
Complete all the judgment details at C. Say how you want the defendant to pay. You can ask for the judgment to be paid by instalments or in one payment. The court will send the defendant an order to pay. You will also be sent a copy.

☐ **I do NOT accept the defendant's proposal for payment**
Complete all the judgment details at C and say how you want the defendant to pay. Give your reasons for objecting to the defendant's offer of payment in the section overleaf. Return this slip to the court **together with the defendant's admission N9A** (or a copy). The court will fix a rate of payment and send the defendant an order to pay. You will also be sent a copy.

I certify that the information given is correct

Signed ...... *E Sprogett* ...... Dated ...... **13/8/98** ......

In the	ANYTOWN	County Court
Case Number *Always quote this*		**98/16254**
Plaintiff	**Mrs E SPROGETT**	
Defendant	**Mr FREDERICK PLUMMER**	
Plaintiff's Ref.		

C Judgment details
I would like the judgment to be paid

☐ (forthwith) *only tick this box if you intend to enforce the order right away*
☐ (by instalments of £ **20.00** per month)
☐ (in full by)

Amount of claim as stated in summons (including interest at date of issue)	450	00
Interest since date of summons (if any) Period .... Rate ....%	–	–
Court fees shown on summons	50	00
Solicitor's costs (if any) on issuing summons	–	–
Sub Total	500	00
Solicitor's costs (if any) on entering judgment	–	–
Sub Total	500	00
Deduct amount (if any) paid since issue	–	–
Amount payable by defendant	500	00

N205A Notice of issue (default summons) and request for judgment (Order 3, rule (2)(d)(1), Order 9 rules 3 and 6)   Dd 8252220 200M 5/91 Ed(289481)

Asking the Chief Clerk of the County Court to enter judgment in default

Dear

[Reference: case number]

I understand that the defendant's failure to file a defence within 14 days of the service of the summons entitles me to enter judgment automatically.

As 14 days have expired since the service of the summons and I have not received a defence, I enclose form N14 (Request for Entry of Judgment in Default Action), together with the case note and would be grateful if you would enter judgment in default accordingly.

Yours sincerely

encs.

Asking the Chief Clerk of the County Court to postpone the preliminary hearing

Dear

[Reference: case number]

I have just received your note of **[date]**, giving a date of **[date]** for the preliminary hearing in this case.

Unfortunately I will not be able to attend on that date because **[reason]**.

I would therefore be grateful if you would fix a new date. I should be able to attend court from **[date]** onwards.

I look forward to hearing from you in due course.

Yours sincerely

Proposing to the defendant that 'directions for trial' be applied to the case

Dear

[Reference: case number]

I have heard from the **[location]** county court with a notice of the preliminary hearing in our case. In an effort to save time and travel expenses, I propose that we do not have a preliminary hearing. I would like to agree directions for trial by post, and suggest the following:

1. Exchange of documents within 14 days.
2. A date be set for trial on the first available day.
3. Expert witnesses be limited to one for each party.
4. Experts' reports be exchanged within seven days of the hearing.
5. We apply to the court for further directions should they be necessary.

If you agree to these directions, please write to me accordingly so that I may copy both your letter and this letter to the court.

Yours sincerely

Asking the defendant to supply copies of documents for inspection

Dear

[Reference: case number]

Thank you for your letter of **[date]**, together with your list of documents.

I would like to inspect the following documents: **[give numbers]**. I understand that it is standard practice for the parties to exchange copies by post and I would ask you to send copies to me direct. I am prepared to meet the cost of postage and photocopying if necessary. I look forward to receiving copies of these documents within seven days.

Please let me know if there are any documents included in my list of documents which you wish to inspect. I will then send you copies. I understand that I am entitled to ask you for the cost of having such copies made.

Yours sincerely

NOTE
Documents are normally exchanged by post. If the defendant asks you to pay postal and photocopying costs you should agree. You, in your turn, are entitled to ask for any expenses you incur in providing the defendant with documents.

Informing the defendant that the case is discontinued following receipt of full and final payment

---

Dear

[Reference: case number]

Thank you for your letter of **[date]** proposing settlement **[describe]**.

I am pleased to accept your cheque for **[£.....]** in full and final settlement of my claim against you.

I am therefore discontinuing my claim against you in the **[location]** County Court and am copying this letter to the court.

Yours sincerely

cc: The Chief Clerk **[location]** County Court

Requiring the defendant to pay the sum agreed by the court

Dear

[Reference: case number]

The adjudication in the above case is that I am to recover from you the sum of **[£.....]** for **[damages etc.]** and **[£.....]** for expenses, amounting to a total of **[£....]**.

Under the terms of the judgment the above sum is payable forthwith.

Unless I receive your cheque for **[total amount]** within seven days I shall issue enforcement proceedings against you. This may result in goods belonging to you being seized and sold to satisfy the judgment and costs.

Yours sincerely

Complaining to the Chief Clerk about court errors

Dear

[Reference: title of case and case number]

I wish to complain about the quality of service I have received from the court staff concerned with the administrative support in the above case.

I am enclosing copies of all the relevant correspondence in the case. As you will see from the file, the court staff have made the following administrative errors when dealing with the case: **[describe]**. The court also fell below the standards set out in the Charter for Court Users as follows: **[describe]**.

I now ask you to investigate this matter, and I look forward to hearing from you in due course.

Yours sincerely

encs.

Chapter 18

Scotland

MOST of the rules which apply when you buy goods and services are broadly the same throughout the UK. For example, if you buy faulty goods or receive a substandard service, you have the same entitlement to redress north and south of the border. Rights covering buying goods in Scotland are covered by the Sale of Goods Act 1979 as they are elsewhere. If you receive a substandard service – faulty building work, damage by a dry-cleaner, photoprocessor, and so on – your rights in Scotland are covered by common law, rather than the Supply of Goods and Services Act 1982, which applies in England and Wales.

But there are some differences. If, for example, you have a manufacturer's guarantee in Scotland which promises to repair any faulty parts, it is legally enforceable, whereas in England and Wales it might not be. This is because certain promises, such as guarantees, are treated as contracts in Scots law – but they might not be in English law. It makes little practical difference though as most manufacturers honour their guarantees anyway, so consumers south of the border are not at a disadvantage.

Small claims

A small claims procedure was introduced in Scotland in 1988. Cases are heard in the Sheriff Court. The main features of the procedure are:

- it can be used for almost all consumer cases up to a value of £750
- all you have to do to start your claim is fill in a simple form and pay a small fee (a Sheriff Clerk will tell you what the fee is)

- there is a strict limit on the bill you are likely to face if your claim is defended. If your claim is for less than £200, there is a 'no expenses' rule – which means you only have to pay your own expenses, win or lose. If you claim more than £200, you will not have to pay more than £75 of the other side's expenses even if you lose
- if your case comes to a hearing, it should be informal. You will not need a solicitor and you will not have to worry about the usual technical rules about the presentation of cases.

If you want to begin an action in Scotland, obtain further information on the small claims procedure by reading the series of leaflets available from your local court – before you proceed.

Chapter 19

Northern Ireland

CONSUMER rights and consumer law in Northern Ireland are virtually identical to those in England and Wales. For instance, shopping, holiday rights and so on, and consumer rights in respect of British Telecom are the same across the United Kingdom. However, there are differences. For example, complaints about electricity and gas are dealt with by the General Consumer Council for Northern Ireland rather than OFFER and OFGAS which cover Britain (see Chapter 9 on Domestic Services, and Addresses at the back of this book). Similarly, in Northern Ireland the equivalent of trading standards departments is the Trading Standards Branch of the Department for Economic Development for Northern Ireland.

Any differences are noted in the preceding chapters dealing with your rights in specific circumstances.

Small claims

A small claims procedure in Northern Ireland is similar to that in the county courts in England and Wales (see Chapter 17). The main differences in the procedure are:

- the small claims court can be used for consumer claims up to £1,000
- the method of dealing with cases is known as 'Arbitration'; the person making the claim is called the 'Applicant' (rather than 'Plaintiff') and the person against whom the claim is made is called the 'Respondent' (rather than 'Defendant')
- small claims are decided by Circuit Registrars, rather than

district judges

- the court fee is currently between £10 and £38, depending on the amount you are claiming.

If you want to bring a small claim in Northern Ireland, obtain further information by reading *Small Claims – Northern Ireland*, a free booklet available from your local Small Claims Court Office (see Addresses at the back of this book). For information on enforcement procedure and fees contact any Small Claims Court Office or the Enforcement of Judgments Office (also listed).

Glossary

Breach of contract A refusal or failure by a party to a contract to fulfil an obligation imposed on him under that contract.

Caveat emptor 'Let the buyer beware.' This legal principle applies to the sale of property, and means that the onus is on the buyer to ascertain the quality and condition of a property before proceeding with its purchase. In this instance, purchasers do not have the right to seek redress subsequently.

Civil law Law which is concerned with rights and duties that pertain to individual citizens. If you suffer loss because someone else transgresses these laws then you have a right to redress and are entitled to take that person to court.

Common law This kind of law is based on the decisions of the courts in actual cases and amounts to the use of precedent.

Contract Any agreement that can be enforced by law. It gives the parties who have made the contract certain rights and obligations. Contracts can be made in writing, by word of mouth or even without a single word being spoken or written. Every day people make contracts without putting them in writing – buying food in supermarkets or travelling by bus, for example. These have the same standing as written contracts and, like all contracts, are governed by the law of contract.

Cooling-off period The interval in which you are legally entitled to cancel a deal or contract without being financially penalised.

Criminal law Law which is concerned with offences against the public, such as the Trade Descriptions Act 1968. Criminal law affecting consumers is enforced by public authorities like Trading Standards Departments. You cannot get compensation directly by reporting a criminal offence such as a false trade description, but it will give you added leverage with your complaint.

Defendant   The person against whom a civil court case is brought (*cf.* plaintiff).

Estimate   A rough, provisional guide to the price that a tradesman will charge once the work is complete.

Fitness for purpose   If you inform a retailer that you want goods for a specific purpose, then as well as being fit for their more general purpose, the goods should also be reasonably fit for the specific purpose. If they are not, you have a claim against the retailer.

Guarantee   A manufacturer's promise to resolve manufacturing problems in its products free of charge. Some offer your money back, others offer a free repair or replacement. Always check the wording of a guarantee to see what is included. Guarantees are in addition to your rights under the Sale of Goods Act and are not in any way an alternative to these rights.

Injunction   A formal court order requiring a person or organisation to do, or not to do, a particular act. If an injunction is not obeyed, the party concerned may be fined or sent to prison. It lasts as long as the court so decrees.

Judgment   The formal decision of a court.

Law of bailment   A common law (*cf.*) rule which applies when you leave goods with another person or body to be kept safely, taken care of by them and returned to you on demand. If goods are lost or damaged while the other person or body has them, they are responsible to compensate you – unless they can prove that the loss or damage was caused through no fault on their part.

Letter before action   A final letter giving the defendant, whether an individual or an organisation, one last opportunity to settle a claim before a summons is issued.

Negligence   The breach of a legal duty to take reasonable care, resulting in damage to the plaintiff.

Nuisance   The unlawful interference with someone else's enjoyment of his home.

Paying under protest   If a purchaser makes it clear, preferably in writing, when paying for goods or services that he or she is 'paying under protest', the purchaser retains the right to bring a claim later if something is wrong, or later goes wrong, with the item or service.

Plaintiff   The person bringing a civil case in court. (*cf.* defendant).

Quotation   A firm indication, given before any work is started, of the price that a tradesman will charge once his work is complete.

Rejecting goods   Indicating to a retailer that the purchaser does not want the goods in question and in accordance with legally defined rights is seeking a refund.

Reasonable   Description used in legislation to give some definition to the period of time within which certain parties have rights to redress. In consumer matters it is used in legislation to describe the time during which goods can be rejected and a full refund demanded. As 'a reasonable time' is not a precise interval, but depends on the circumstances of each case, it is advisable for consumers to act to seek redress as soon as they can.

Reserving rights   Preserving the consumer's right, in letters or in verbal complaint, to bring a subsequent claim, if the problem is not resolved at this stage.

Satisfactory quality   A legal requirement that goods should work properly, be free from minor defects, safe, durable and, if new, look new and be in good condition.

Statute law   Legislation which consists of Acts of Parliament (for example, the Sale of Goods Act 1979) and Regulations and Orders made under the general authority of Acts of Parliament.

Summons   A formal document issued by a court informing a defendant that a court case has been started and instructing him to do something, such as defend the case or pay a sum of money to the plaintiff.

Time is of the essence   An expression used in contracts to make time a crucial element of that contract and entitle the consumer to cancel it and insist on a full refund of the price paid if goods are not delivered in accordance with these instructions, or if a service is not performed on time.

Without prejudice   A term added to documents, usually letters, which attempts to protect the writer from having the letter construed as an admission of liability or willingness to settle. Generally, nothing said in 'without prejudice' correspondence will be allowed in evidence should the matter come to court. It should not be used on any documentation which may be needed to prove a case, should the lack of appropriate response to a complaint mean that the issue is taken to court.

Addresses

MANY trade and professional bodies operate codes of practice which regulate the handling of complaints against their members; some also administer arbitration schemes. We list below some of the Ombudsmen, organisations and associations to whom you should address your complaints in particular circumstances. Your local Citizens Advice Bureau or library will have details of others.

Arbitration

Chartered Institute of Arbitrators
24 Angel Gate, City Road,
London EC1V 2RS
Tel: 0171-837 4483
Fax: 0171-837 4185

Banks

Association for Payment Clearing Services
Mercury House, Triton Court,
14 Finsbury Square,
London EC2A 1BR
Tel: 0171-711 6234
Fax: 0171-711 6276
Web site: http://www.apacs.org.uk

Banking Ombudsman
70 Gray's Inn Road, London
WC1X 8NB
Tel: 0171-404 9944
Fax: 0171-405 5052
Email:
banking.ombudsman@obo.org.uk

Builders

Federation of Master Builders
14 Great James Street, London
WC1N 3DP
Tel: 0171-242 7583
Fax: 0171-404 0296

Joint Contract Tribunal
82 New Cavendish Street,
London W1M 8AD
Tel: 0171-580 5588
Fax: 0171-323 1590

National House Building Council
Buildmark House, Chiltern
Avenue, Amersham HP6 5AP
Tel: (01494) 434477
Fax: (01494) 728521

Building societies

Building Societies Ombudsman
Millbank Tower, Millbank,
London SW1P 4XS
Tel: 0171-931 0044
Fax: 0171-931 8485

Cars

Institute of Automotive Engineer Assessors
Stowe House, Netherstowe,
Lichfield, Staffordshire WS13 6TJ
Tel: (01543) 251346
Fax: (01543) 415804
Email:
iaea@ismstowe.demon.co.uk

Retail Motor Industry Federation
201 Great Portland Street,
London W1N 6AB
Tel: 0171-580 9122

Scottish Motor Trade Association
3 Palmerston Place,
Edinburgh EH12 5AF
Tel: 0131-225 3643
Fax: 0131-220 0446

Domestic services

Electricity
Office of Electricity Regulation (OFFER)
Hagley House, 83-85 Hagley
Road, Birmingham B16 8QG
Tel: 0121-456 2100
Fax: 0121-456 4664
Email: enquiries@
offer-library.demon.co.uk

General Consumer Council for Northern Ireland
Elizabeth House, 116 Holywood
Road, Belfast BT4 1NY
Tel: (01232) 672488
Fax: (01232) 657701
Email: gcc@nics.gov.uk
Web site: http://www.nics.
gov.uk/gcc

Gas
CORGI (Council for Registered Gas Installers)
1 Elmwood, Chineham Business
Park, Crockford Lane,
Basingstoke RG24 8WG
Tel: (01256) 372300
Fax: (01256) 708144

British Gas Services Area Service Centres
Staines Area Service Centre, 30
The Causeway, Staines TW18 3BY
Tel: (01784) 874000
Fax: (01784) 874100

Uddingston Area Service Centre,
Bothwell Road, Uddingston,
Glasgow G71 7TW
Tel: (01698) 819399
Fax: (01698) 819298

Dudley Area Service Centre,
Constitution Hill,
Dudley DY2 8RR
Tel: (01384) 459459
Fax: (01384) 459111

Leeds Area Service Centre, Canal
Street, New Wortley,
Leeds LS12 2UE
Tel: 0113-244 2341
Fax: 0113-254 4467

Stockport Area Service Centre,
Newbridge Lane, Stockport
SK1 2HQ
Tel: 0161-480 7933
Fax: 0161-474 1947

Swindon Area Service Centre,
Ridgeway House, Gipsy Lane,
Swindon SN2 6DB
Tel: (01793) 512444
Fax: (01793) 425540

Leicester Area Service Centre,
Aylestone Road LE2 7QH
Tel: 0116-254 9414
Fax: 0116-247 3446

Web site for all the above:
http://www.service.britgas.co.uk

Gas Consumers Council
Abford House, 15 Wilton Road,
London SW1V 1LT
Tel: 0171-931 0977F
Fax: 0171-630 9934
Email: gcc@gcchead1.sonnet.co.uk

Office of Gas Supply (OFGAS)
Stockley House, 130 Wilton Road,
London SW1V 1LQ
Tel: 0171-828 0898
Fax: 0171-932 1600
Web site:
http://www.ofgas.gov.uk

Telephones
**Office of Telecommunications
(OFTEL)**
50 Ludgate Hill, London
EC4M 7JJ
Tel: 0171-634 8700
Fax: 0171-634 8943
Web site: http://www.oftel.gov.uk

Water
Office of Water Services (OFWAT)
Centre City Tower, 7 Hill Street,
Birmingham B5 4UA
Tel: 0121-625 1300
Fax: 0121-625 1400
Email: A026@cityscope.co.uk
Web site:
http://www.open.gov.uk/ofwat

**Scottish Water and Sewerage
Customers' Council**
Ochil House, Springkerse Business
Park, Stirling FK7 7XE
Tel: (01786) 430200
Fax: (01786) 462018

Double glazing

Glass and Glazing Federation
44-48 Borough High Street,
London SE1 1XB
Tel: 0171-403 7177
Fax: 0171-357 7458

Dry-cleaning

Textile Services Association
7 Churchill Court, 58 Station
Road, North Harrow HA2 7SA
Tel: 0181-863 7755
Fax: 0181-861 2115

Estate agents

**National Association of Estate
Agents**
Arbon House, 21 Jury Street,
Warwick CV34 4EH
Tel: (01926) 496800
Fax: (01926) 400953
Email: naea@dial.pipex.com
Web site:
http://www.propertylive.co.uk

Office of the Ombudsman for Corporate Estate Agents
Beckett House, 4 Bridge Street,
Salisbury SP1 2LX
Tel: (01722) 333306
Fax: (01722) 332296

Health

Commissioner for Complaints
Freepost, Belfast BT1 6BR
Tel: (01232) 233821
Fax: (01232) 234912
Email: ombudsman@nics.gov.uk

General Medical Council
178 Great Portland Street, London
W1N 6JE
Tel: 0171-580 7642
Fax: 0171-915 3641

Health Service Commissioner
Millbank Tower, Millbank,
London SW1P 4QP
Tel: 0171-276 2035
Fax: 0171-217 4000

Health Service Commissioner for Scotland
28 Thistle Street, Edinburgh
EH2 1EN
Tel: 0131-225 7465
Fax: 0131-226 4447
Web site:
http://www.ombudsman.org.uk

Health Service Commissioner for Wales
Fifth Floor, Pearl Assurance House,
Greyfriars Road, Cardiff CF1 3AG
Tel: (01222) 394621
Fax: (01222) 226909

Dentists
General Dental Council
37 Wimpole Street, London
W1M 8DQ
Tel: 0171-486 2171
Fax: 0171-224 3294

Opticians
General Optical Council
41 Harley Street, London
W1N 2DJ
Tel: 0171-580 3898

Holidays

Association of British Travel Agents (ABTA)
55-57 Newman Street, London
W1P 4AH
Tel: 0171-637 2444
Fax: 0171-637 0713
Infoline: (0891) 202520
Web site: http://www.abtanet.com

Insurance

Institute of Public Loss Assessors
14 Red Lion Street, Chesham
HP5 1HB
Tel: (01494) 782342
Fax: (01494) 774928

Insurance Ombudsman Bureau
135 Park Street, London SE1 9EA
Tel: 0171-928 7600
Fax: 0171-902 8197

Mail order

The Direct Marketing Association UK Ltd
Haymarket House, 1 Oxendon Street, London SW1Y 4EE
Tel: 0171-321 2525
Fax: 0171-321 0191
Email: dma@dma.org.uk

Mailing Preference Service
Freepost 22, London W1E 7EZ
Tel: 0171-766 4410
Fax: 0171-976 1886
Email: mps@dma.org.uk

Mail Order Protection Scheme (MOPS)
16 Tooks Court, London EC4A 1LB
Tel: 0171-405 6806
Fax: 0171-404 0106

Mail Order Traders' Association
40 Waterloo Road, Southport PR8 2NG
Tel: (01704) 563787
Fax: (01704) 551247
Email: malcolm landau@compuserve.com

Newspaper Publishers' Association Ltd
34 Southwark Bridge Road, London SE1 9EU
Tel: 0171-928 6928
Tax: 0171-928 2067

Newspaper Society
Bloomsbury House, 74-77 Great Russell Street, London WC1B 3DA
Tel: 0171-636 7014
Fax: 0171-631 5119
Web site: http://www.jicreg.co.uk

Scottish Daily Newspaper Society
48 Palmerston Place, Edinburgh EH12 5DE
Tel: 0131-220 4353
Fax: 0131-220 4344

Scottish Newspapers Publishers' Association
48 Palmerston Place, Edinburgh EH12 5DE
Tel: 0131-220 4353
Fax: 0131-220 4344

Northern Ireland

Enforcement of Judgments Office
7th Floor, Bedford House, 15-22 Bedford Street, Belfast BT2 7DS
Tel: (01232) 245081
Fax: (01232) 313520

Small Claims Court Offices:
ARMAGH
Court Office, Courthouse, The Mall, Armagh BT61 9DJ
Tel: (01861) 522816
Fax: (01861) 528194

BALLYMENA
Court Office, Courthouse, Albert Place, Ballymena BT43 5BS
Tel: (01266) 49416
Fax: (01266) 655371

BELFAST
Belfast County Court, Old Town Hall Building,
80 Victoria Street, Belfast BT1 3FA
Tel: (01232) 326260
Fax: (01232) 313771

CRAIGAVON
Court Office, Courthouse, Central
Way, Craigavon BT64 1AP
Tel: (01762) 341324
Fax: (01762) 341243

DOWNPATRICK
Court Office, Courthouse, 21
English Street, Downpatrick
BT30 6AB
Tel: (01396) 614621
Fax: (01396) 613969

ENNISKILLEN
Petty Sessions Office, Courthouse,
17 East Bridge Street,
Enniskillen BT74 7BW
Tel: (01365) 322356
Fax: (01365) 323636

LONDONDERRY
Crown and County Court Office,
Courthouse, Bishop Street,
Londonderry BT48 6PY
Tel: (01504) 363448
Fax: (01504) 372059

NEWTOWNARDS
Court Office, Courthouse, 3
Regent Street, Newtownards
BT23 4LP
Tel: (01247) 814343
Fax: (01247) 818024

OMAGH
Court Office, Courthouse, High
Street, Omagh BT78 1DU
Tel: (01662) 242056
Fax: (01662) 251198

Pensions

Pensions Ombudsman
11 Belgrave Road, London
SW1V 1RB
Tel: 0171-834 9144
Fax: 0171-821 0065

Removal companies

British Association of Removers
3 Churchill Court, 58 Station
Road, North Harrow HA2 7SA
Tel: 0181-861 3331
Fax: 0181-861 3332

Solicitors

Law Society of England and Wales
113 Chancery Lane, London
WC2A 1PL
Tel: 0171-242 1222
Fax: 0171-831 0344

Law Society of Northern Ireland
Law Society House, 98 Victoria
Street, Belfast BT1 3JZ
Tel: (01232) 231614
Fax: (01232) 232606

Law Society of Scotland
26 Drumsheugh Gardens,
Edinburgh EH3 7YR
Tel: 0131-226 7411
Fax: 0131-225 2934
Email: lawscot@lawscot.org.uk

Legal Services Ombudsman
22 Oxford Court, Oxford Street,
Manchester M2 3WQ
Tel: 0161-236 9532
Fax: 0161-236 2651

Scottish Legal Services Ombudsman
2 Greenside Lane, Edinburgh
EH1 3AH
Tel: 0131-556 5574
Fax: 0131-556 1519

Office for the Supervision of
Solicitors
Victoria Court, 8 Dormer Place,
Leamington Spa CV32 5AE
Tel: (01926) 820082
Fax: (01926) 431435

Surveyors

Incorporated Society of Valuers and
Auctioneers
3 Cadogan Gate, London
SW1X 0AS
Tel: 0171-235 2282
Fax: 0171-235 4390
Web site: http://www.isva.co.uk

Royal Institution of Chartered
Surveyors
12 Great George Street, London
SW1P 3AD
Tel: 0171-222 7000
Fax: 0171-222 9430

Other

Office of Fair Trading
15-25 Bream's Buildings, London
EC4A 1PR
Tel: 0171-211 8000
Fax: 0171-211 8800
Web site:
http://www.open.gov.uk/oft/
ofthome.htm

Commission for Local
Administration in Scotland
23 Walker Street, Edinburgh
EH3 7HX
Tel: 0131-225 5300
Fax: 0131-225 9495

Index

040-933-1